Toward a New, Praxis-Oriented Missiology

American Society of Missiology
Monograph Series

Series Editor, James R. Krabill

The ASM Monograph Series provides a forum for publishing quality dissertations and studies in the field of missiology. Collaborating with Pickwick Publications—a division of Wipf and Stock Publishers of Eugene, Oregon—the American Society of Missiology selects high quality dissertations and other monographic studies that offer research materials in mission studies for scholars, mission and church leaders, and the academic community at large. The ASM seeks scholarly work for publication in the series that throws light on issues confronting Christian world mission in its cultural, social, historical, biblical, and theological dimensions.

Missiology is an academic field that brings together scholars whose professional training ranges from doctoral-level preparation in areas such as Scripture, history and sociology of religions, anthropology, theology, international relations, interreligious interchange, mission history, inculturation, and church law. The American Society of Missiology, which sponsors this series, is an ecumenical body drawing members from Independent and Ecumenical Protestant, Catholic, Orthodox, and other traditions. Members of the ASM are united by their commitment to reflect on and do scholarly work relating to both mission history and the present-day mission of the church. The ASM Monograph Series aims to publish works of exceptional merit on specialized topics, with particular attention given to work by younger scholars, the dissemination and publication of which is difficult under the economic pressures of standard publishing models.

Persons seeking information about the ASM or the guidelines for having their dissertations considered for publication in the ASM Monograph Series should consult the Society's website—www.asmweb.org.

Members of the ASM Monograph Committee who approved this book are:

Paul V. Kollman, Associate Professor of Theology and Executive Director Center for Social Concerns (CSC), University of Notre Dame

William P. Gregory, Associate Professor of Religious Studies, Clarke University

RECENTLY PUBLISHED IN THE ASM MONOGRAPH SERIES

L. Lynn Thigpen, *Connected Learning: How Adults with Limited Formal Education Learn*

Craig S. Hendrickson, *Charismatic Leadership and Missional Change: Mission-Actional Ministry in a Multiethnic Church*

Toward a New, Praxis-Oriented Missiology

Rediscovering Paulo Freire's Concept of Conscientização *and Enhancing Christian Mission as Prophetic Dialogue*

Rosalia Meza, VDMF

American Society of Missiology Monograph
Series vol. 46

☙PICKWICK *Publications* • Eugene, Oregon

TOWARD A NEW, PRAXIS-ORIENTED MISSIOLOGY
Rediscovering Paulo Freire's Concept of *Conscientização*
and Enhancing Christian Mission as Prophetic Dialogue

American Society of Missiology Monograph Series 46

Copyright © 2020 Rosalia Meza. All rights reserved. Except for brief quotations in critical publications or reviews, no part of this book may be reproduced in any manner without prior written permission from the publisher. Write: Permissions, Wipf and Stock Publishers, 199 W. 8th Ave., Suite 3, Eugene, OR 97401.

Pickwick Publications
An Imprint of Wipf and Stock Publishers
199 W. 8th Ave., Suite 3
Eugene, OR 97401

www.wipfandstock.com

PAPERBACK ISBN: 978-1-7252-5823-5
HARDCOVER ISBN: 978-1-7252-5824-2
EBOOK ISBN: 978-1-7252-5825-9

Cataloguing-in-Publication data:

Names: Meza, Rosalia, author.

Title: Toward a new, praxis-oriented missiology : rediscovering Paulo Freire's Concept of *Conscientização* and enhancing christian mission as prophetic dialogue / by Rosalia Meza.

Description: Eugene, OR: Pickwick Publications, 2020 | American Society of Missiology Monograph Series 46 | Includes bibliographical references and index.

Identifiers: ISBN 978-1-7252-5823-5 (paperback) | ISBN 978-1-7252-5824-2 (hardcover) | ISBN 978-1-7252-5825-9 (ebook)

Subjects: LCSH: Freire, Paulo, 1921—1997 | Missions—Theory

Classification: BV2183 M49 2020 (print) | BV2183 (ebook)

Manufactured in the U.S.A.   06/16/20

To my mother and father,

Rosalía Moreno de Meza
(1949–2007)

and

Víctor Meza Lozano
(1949–2007),

who were great examples of
faith and authenticity.

Contents

Illustrations | ix
Acknowledgments | xi
Abbreviations | xiii
Introduction | xv

1. Understanding of Mission as Prophetic Dialogue | 1
   The Church and Mission since the Second Vatican Council | 2
   Who Is Stephen B. Bevans? | 6
   Mission as Prophetic Dialogue | 7
   Mission as Dialogue | 10
   Mission as Prophecy | 12
   Contextual Theology and Prophetic Dialogue | 15
   Exercising Prophetic Dialogue | 19
   What Does Prophetic Dialogue Have to Offer to the Twenty-First-Century Church? | 21
   Concluding Thoughts | 24

2. Paulo Freire's Concept of *Conscientização*: A Commitment to Process | 27
   Who Is Paulo Freire? | 28
   Freire's Philosophical Influence | 29
   What Is *Conscientização*? | 34

Contents

    The Why and How of *Conscientização* | 36
    Freire's Understanding of Reality | 44
    What Are the Aims of Freire's *Conscientização*? | 49
    Conscientização and Dialogue | 54
    Concluding Thoughts | 57

3. *Conscientização* Enhances Prophetic Dialogue and Vice Versa | 60
    Historical Awareness of Missionary Methods | 61
    Transmission of Christian Faith | 67
    Bevans and Freire | 73
    Common Aspects in Bevans's and Freire's Thought | 77
    Concluding Thoughts | 81

4. Contribution to the Praxis and Field of Missiology in Light of Contemporary Verbum Dei Missionary Fraternity Vision and Ministry | 83
    The Verbum Dei Missionary Fraternity Charism and Mission | 84
    Central Elements in VDMF Mission | 90
    A Growing Area in VDMF Mission | 97
    Folding into the Concepts of Prophetic Dialogue and *Conscientização* | 101
    Concluding Thoughts | 108

Conclusion | 111

Bibliography | 121

Index | 129

Illustrations

FIGURES

2.1. Freire's phases to pre-literacy and post-literacy. | 43

2.2. Freire's understanding of dialogue and anti-dialogue. | 55

3.1. Common elements in prophetic dialogue and *conscientização*. | 80

4.1. Wheel of Metanoia. From Prinz, *Endangering Hunger for God*, fig. 4. | 92

4.2. Prophetic dialogue, *conscientização*, and Verbum Dei charism connecting. | 108

TABLE

3.1. Common elements in prophetic dialogue and *conscientização*. | 78

Acknowledgments

This work would not have been possible without the many people who inspired, supported, and guided me to be the best me. Writing this work has had a very positive impact on me. It has allowed me to listen and find my own voice as a young Catholic woman religious, to acknowledge God's grace, to continue the unfolding of my vocation through my work with a very vulnerable population in California, and to interweave the main elements that keep my passion and religious vocation alive.

I begin by acknowledging all the people who supported and helped me to make this possible: to all of you, many thanks. First and foremost, I thank God because this work was possible through God's grace, which made me see the transcendence of my dedication to mission and the gift of the Verbum Dei charism through the experience of my research and writing. I also thank Rev. Jaime Bonet Bonet, the founder of my religious community, for his passion to transmit in a kerygmatic way the essence of the gospel, which I had the privilege to witness in his life and have been able to absorb and assimilate over the last twenty years of my life.

I offer my deep gratitude and appreciation to Dr. Eduardo Fernandez, SJ, for encouraging me to develop this work. Special thanks also to Dr. Stephen Bevans, SVD. I feel humbled and honored that Steve not only allowed me to use his work on *prophetic dialogue* but also accepted to participate in this project. In addition, I offer my deep gratitude to Drs. Margaret Guider, OSF, and Julia Prinz, VDMF. Thank you for being wonderful mentors who challenged my theological thinking.

Acknowledgments

I would also like to thank the sisters of my community for the many ways they have been supporting me and being family for me. Also, very special thanks to Melanio Puzon, my proofreader. I would also like to thank the Latino immigrant people in northern and southern California who have been part of my life for the last twenty years. I have learned and been inspired and uplifted by the many life stories that contain so much pain and suffering but also so much faith, hope, and joy.

Una profunda gratitud a toda mi familia (los Meza y los Moreno) y mis amigas de toda la vida, especialmente a Edgar Marín Meza, mi hermano, y su familia y a la Tirringa (mi abuelita) por su gran entereza y fe ante los dolores de la vida. Ella ha perdido cuatro de sus hijos y dos de ellos de una forma muy trágica (una de ellas es mi mamá). De mi abuelita he adquirido mi mayor aprendizaje teológico. Gracias por todo su apoyo no sólo en mis estudios pero principalmente por seguir creyendo y apoyando en mi vocación ahora en la ausencia de mis padres.

Finalmente, termino con mi más profundo agradecimiento a mi papá, Víctor Meza, y a mi mamá, Rosalía Meza, que están en el cielo y que estarían muy orgullosos de su hija. Los extraño mucho, a los dos muchas gracias por su vida y por todo lo que pude aprender de ustedes, es la mejor herencia que me han dejado.

Abbreviations

CELAM	Consejo Episcopal Latinoamericano (Latin American Episcopal Conference)
CTU	Catholic Theological Union, Chicago, IL
FABC	Federation of Asian Bishops' Conferences
NFCL	New Form of Consecrated Life
SESI	Serviço Social da Indústria
SVD	Society of the Divine Word
UNESCO	United Nations Educational, Scientific, and Cultural Organization
VDMF	Verbum Dei Missionary Fraternity

Introduction

As a student of pedagogy, I have been profoundly challenged and enriched by Paulo Freire's work. The publication of *Pedagogy of the Oppressed* (1970) made Freire an icon of social change through education. His pedagogical work was written in and reflected the context of a Third World reality. Its main focus was to liberate those who suffer from economic poverty and intellectual ignorance as well as political and cultural exclusion in Brazil.

Freire's revolutionary pedagogical work intends to lead the person into a process of *conscientização*. For him, *conscientização* is a process that helps the person attain awareness of oppressive sociocultural dynamics with the capacity to transform them. This process involves action and reflection, and it advocates for the capacity to not only understand oneself but also others. This understanding is key to transforming, reordering, and reconciling relationships. Moreover, *conscientização* creates the conditions for an authentic dialogue, which involves respect and openness. Dialogue should not involve one person acting on another but rather people working with each other.[1] "Dialogue cannot be reduced to the act of one person's 'depositing' ideas in another, nor can it become a simple exchange of ideas to be 'consumed' by the discussants."[2] Therefore, if *conscientização* is disengaged from the process of dialogue, it cannot in and of itself lead to any kind of transformation. In other words, Freire's concept of *conscientização* is founded upon a dialectical and phenomenological approach to consciousness and the world. It requires intentionality, affirmation of the subjective-objective

1. See Freire, *Pedagogy of Freedom*, 65.
2. Freire, *Pedagogy of the Oppressed*, 89.

Introduction

dialectic, consciousness, as well as the capacity to act consciously on the objectivized reality.[3] It also requires dialogue understood as an act of creation; it must not serve as a crafty instrument for the domination of one person by another.[4] Freire's pedagogy aims at initiating a transformative process of knowledge which leads to the changing of social structures. This process of transformation is not guaranteed when other forces and power dynamics impede, compete with, or subvert the process because these dynamics make dialogue impossible.

Furthermore, looking at the current discourse in missiology, there are new and different frontiers and factors that are reshaping the meaning of mission. Christian mission today is in search of new directions to approach the postmodern, postcolonial, and ecumenical paradigms.[5] Regardless of the diversity within this discourse, there is a common understanding about the need to be sensitive to thought and to cultural, social, political, spiritual, and contextual movements of the present time, or as the Second Vatican Council put it, "to read the signs of the times."[6] Therefore, mission is not just an enterprise to bring Christ and the gospel to the people (in the case of a Christian approach); it is a conscious dedication, preparation, and commitment to incarnate the gospel in every culture not only individually but in specific societies. An open attitude, that is, an openness to dialogue, must characterize the interior disposition of the persons undertaking holistically this kind of mission.[7]

Upon reflecting on my years of ministry as a Catholic religious missionary sister of the Verbum Dei Missionary Fraternity, especially with the Latino immigrant population in California, I have come to realize the importance of Freire's work for ministry. His pedagogy supports this conscious dedication, preparation, dialogue, and commitment to incarnate the gospel in every culture. Moreover, it is concerned about fomenting an interior attitude in which the goal is to read, interpret, and intervene in the specific realities of people's experience. Using Freire's concept of *conscientização*, encompassed with his understanding of dialogue, I wish to argue that mission is not just the transmission of knowledge that keeps an established structure and culture alive (often justified and glorified by a

3. Freire, "Conscientisation," 23.
4. Freire, *Pedagogy of the Oppressed*, 89.
5. See Scherer and Bevans, *Theological Foundations*; Bosch, *Transforming Mission*.
6. Second Vatican Council, *Gaudium et Spes*, 4.
7. See Dorr, *Mission in Today's World*, 193.

Introduction

specific ecclesiological model). Rather, mission aims at the process of embodying the content and praxis of the gospel. Mission can be understood as an invitation to initiate a transformative process of faith, which leads into personal and social transformation.

During my study of missiology, I found myself particularly drawn to the holistic concept of mission advanced by Stephen Bevans and Roger Schroeder, especially that of *prophetic dialogue*. Although both introduced the concept of prophetic dialogue, Bevans has developed it further in his own individual work. He describes prophetic dialogue in the following way:

> Mission is about preaching, serving and witnessing to the work of God in our world; it is about living and working as partners with God in the patient yet unwearied work of inviting and persuading women and men to enter into relationship with their world, with one another, and with Godself. Mission is dialogue. It takes people where they are; it is open to their traditions and culture and experience; it recognizes the validity of their own religious existence and the integrity of their own religious ends. But it is *prophetic* dialogue because it calls people beyond; it calls people to conversion; it calls people to deeper and fuller truth that can only be found in communion with dialogue's Trinitarian ground.[8]

Therefore, prophetic dialogue encounters the other where they are in their cultural context and religious experience and comes into a relationship with the other, with their world, and with God. Also, it helps discern a way forward, a call to go beyond. In my own ministry, prophetic dialogue has allowed me to meet the Latino immigrant people where they are in their process of faith. The approach is not one of imposing doctrine but rather an invitation to go beyond and to spark a transformative process from where they are.

This work proposes to bring into dialogue Freire's concept of *conscientização* and the notion of mission as prophetic dialogue. Following Freire's legacy, my intention is not to import Freire's pedagogy to mission but to recover the inherent process in those two concepts that lead to a potential transformation in the person and society.[9]

---

8. Stephen Bevans, e-mail to author, November 1, 2015.

9. Freire was always against importing or exporting his pedagogical practices. Instead, he insisted that his ideas be recreated, reinvented, and rewritten. See Araújo Freire and Macedo, *Paulo Freire Reader*, 6.

Introduction

SCOPE AND NATURE

Within his educational thought and philosophy, I will elaborate on Freire's concept of *conscientização*, which is not only at the heart of his pedagogy but also interwoven into all his works. I will introduce the concept of *conscientização* and its encompassing relationship with dialogue for further development in mission theology and praxis. As mentioned above, *conscientização* supports the conscious dedication, preparation, dialogue, and commitment to incarnate the gospel in every culture. It sets up the interior attitude to read, interpret, as well as intervene in specific realities.

Likewise, this work will be limited to understanding mission as prophetic dialogue. As mentioned earlier, this concept was introduced by Bevans and Schroeder, but Bevans developed it further. For this reason, I will focus more on Bevans's work. I will introduce the reader to the riches that prophetic dialogue offers to mission praxis. With the help of Bevans's work and other missiologists, I will also explore questions and challenges in missiological discourse today, such as how to promote the gospel in a more experiential way.

The analysis of my praxis will show the experiential and transformative elements of the Verbum Dei charism applied to my ministry with the Latino immigrant population in California. This analysis will be grounded in the writings of Rev. Jaime Bonet Bonet, founder of the Verbum Dei community. I will also look at the writings of other members of Verbum Dei to examine the spirituality and tools with which I am exercising my ministry. I will use Bevans's and Freire's work to demonstrate the effectiveness of the concepts of prophetic dialogue and *conscientização* in the Verbum Dei Missionary Fraternity mission praxis.

OBJECTIVE OF THIS WORK

This work will bring into dialogue the notion of mission as prophetic dialogue and Freire's concept of *conscientização*. My aim is not to use Freire's *conscientização* as a method to do mission but to rescue the process that leads to transformation in both concepts, allowing one to encounter the other where they are while respecting the uniqueness of every person, culture, church, and society. Prophetic dialogue, enriched by Freire's thought and vice versa, can open new perspectives within missiology and provide a new approach to mission praxis.

Introduction

METHODOLOGY

Throughout the whole work, the reader will perceive that the methodology used intends to rescue elements that are experiential. These elements form the engine for a participatory process of faith and societal transformation. This will be presented by tracing the development of the concept of prophetic dialogue and *conscientização* by first introducing the concept of mission as prophetic dialogue within the tradition and magisterium of the Catholic Church and its relevance for understanding mission in the twenty-first century. Second, I will analyze and present the concept of *conscientização*, paying special attention to Freire's biographical approach, and the philosophical influences which caused Freire to approach *conscientização* as a process. Third, I will evaluate how far and by what means Freire's work on *conscientização* can be compared and enriched by Bevans's work on prophetic dialogue and vice versa. Finally, I will examine the missiological implications regarding a praxis approach toward integrating these two helpful concepts, thereby demonstrating its effectiveness in my pastoral work among Latino immigrants in California, its presence in the Verbum Dei charism, and the basis for exercising my Verbum Dei ministry.

SIGNIFICANCE

My aim is to provide the reader a creative way to grasp the process of active participation that makes the transmission of faith experiential, to show how prophetic dialogue enhances *conscientização* and vice versa, and to demonstrate that the thought of Bevans and Freire on this topic can be very helpful for transmitting the faith more experientially and contextually, which is necessary for mission praxis today. Moreover, what made me aware of the unique connection between prophetic dialogue and *conscientização* is Verbum Dei's charism. Nascent during the period leading up to the Second Vatican Council, this charism centers on the kerygmatic transmission of the gospel in its essence leads to social transformation and dialogical participatory mission praxis.

This book contributes to mission theology by providing a new approach to mission praxis understood as an invitation to initiate a transformative process of faith and awareness in societies rather than the static transmission of a specifically formulated Christian content of faith.[10] More-

---

10. Dr. Julia Prinz, former VDMF US Provincial and member of my doctoral dissertation committee, reminded me that my work is not simply integrating a deposit of faith with human experience in mission praxis but rather practicing "'deep listening'

Introduction

over, to my knowledge, introducing such a challenging and extraordinary treatment of such a pedagogical process has not yet been used in mission theology or practice and is therefore unique in its contribution. My hope is to broaden the mission theoretical discourse as well as to animate and challenge the praxis of mission. I will show that the Christian understanding of mission is not just an enterprise to bring Christ and the gospel to the people but is a conscious dedication, preparation, dialogue, and commitment to incarnate the gospel for the individual and societal structures. This aim requires a holistic vision furthered by true dialogue, one aimed at working toward an "ortho-praxis."[11]

STRUCTURE

The provided structure for this work will safeguard the inherent process of active participation in the concepts of prophetic dialogue and *conscientização*, which support faith transmission that is experiential.

Chapter 1 will introduce the concept of mission and the self-understanding of the church after the Second Vatican Council. This introduction will provide the context for appreciating the concept of prophetic dialogue. The chapter will give Stephen Bevans's background followed by an analysis of his vision of mission as prophetic dialogue. Next, the chapter will describe the understanding of prophetic dialogue as contextual theology. Finally, the chapter will show an example of prophetic dialogue in a concrete ministerial context and its relevance in the twenty-first century.

Chapter 2 will provide a brief biography of Freire and examine his philosophical influences. This will provide a framework for analyzing his concept of *conscientização*. This chapter will examine *conscientização* and explain why and how it is integral to Freire's pedagogy. The chapter will also describe his philosophical understanding of reality in order to provide an understanding of the aims of *conscientização*. The chapter will conclude by emphasizing the importance of dialogue in the process of *conscientização*.

Chapter 3 will present the historical awareness of missionary methods in order to show the relevance of the pedagogical implications of *conscientização* and prophetic dialogue. The chapter will examine the role of experience as it relates to the transmission of the Christian faith. The

in experience, biography, and narrative [which] embodies faith or possibly unfolds/ *despliega* the very faith in the individual and community." Julia Prinz, e-mail to author, April 24, 2018.

11. See "Praxis Model" in Bevans, *Models of Contextual Theology*, 70–79.

Introduction

chapter will also evaluate how far and by what means Freire's work on *conscientização* can enrich Bevans's work on prophetic dialogue and vice versa. The chapter will close by presenting some common aspects in Bevans's and Freire's thought.

Chapter 4 will present the Verbum Dei Missionary Fraternity's charism and central elements of its mission, using my ministerial work with the Latino immigrant population. The chapter will also bridge the concepts of prophetic dialogue and *conscientização* and show that the integration of both concepts reveals how a person is led into a process of participatory transformation. Special attention will be given to describe how this process creates social change while respecting the uniqueness of every person, culture, church, and society. The chapter will conclude by presenting the connection of the VDMF charism with Bevans's and Freire's work.

Finally, by way of conclusion, the contribution of Bevans's and Freire's work in the field of missiology will be presented. It will show that the new insights derived from this work include tools for conscious transmission of the Christian faith in a more experiential and participatory way with the boldness to humbly approach mission barefooted. Though not affecting the substance of this research, some questions will be considered from what remains regarding Bevans's prophetic dialogue and Freire's *conscientização*. The conclusion will end with a future perspective for a better understanding of the church herself through a deeper understanding of the church's mission.

1

Understanding of Mission as Prophetic Dialogue

> Mission is not primarily an activity of the church, but an attribute of God.
>
> —DAVID J. BOSCH, *TRANSFORMING MISSION*

THIS CHAPTER WILL DISCUSS the concept of mission as prophetic dialogue by following its development from the joint work of Stephen Bevans and Roger Schroeder to Bevans's own individual work. In order to show how Bevans developed this concept, the chapter will present the context within which his notion of mission as prophetic dialogue unfolded and then break up the concept into two terms: mission as dialogue and mission as prophecy. Subsequently, the chapter will introduce Bevans's concept of prophetic dialogue as contextual theology and its relevance to engage mission contextually. Lastly, the chapter will demonstrate the relevance of understanding mission as prophetic dialogue in twenty-first-century missiological discourse.

To better contextualize Bevans's work, this chapter will begin by offering a brief presentation on how the church's understanding of mission has shifted since the Second Vatican Council, which opened under the pontificate of Pope John XXIII on October 11, 1962, and closed under Pope Paul VI on the Feast of the Immaculate Conception on December 8, 1965.

Toward a New, Praxis-Oriented Missiology

THE CHURCH AND MISSION SINCE THE SECOND VATICAN COUNCIL

Looking at the current discourse in missiology, there are new and different frontiers and factors that are reshaping the understanding of mission and evangelization. Christian mission is faced with issues, and it is invited to grow in directions that are opening up new paradigms of theology and ministry. Therefore, the work of mission and evangelization is moving in new directions.[1] Our task is to be good listeners to our contexts and to the needs of the world so that we allow a narrative of communion and inclusion to emerge in the church and continue collaborating in the *missio Dei* (mission of God).[2]

Vietnamese American theologian Peter C. Phan observed that mission is "not an innocent word."[3] In the name of mission, harm has been done to peoples and cultures throughout the world. The words "mission" and "missionaries" often carries a negative connotation of violence, imposition, destruction of cultures, and colonialism. Nevertheless, thanks to the Second Vatican Council and subsequent theological reflections by theologians, missiologists, ecclesiologists, and other interdisciplinary experts, such a perspective has been challenged. We can no longer think of mission, for example, as the only way of saving souls. We now say that salvation is possible outside explicit faith in Jesus Christ.[4] We cannot conceive of mission as going from the West to the rest of the world. Nor do we generally employ military language such as "conquering the world for Christ."[5] Our theology of mission has significantly changed and now takes more into account the changes in the social, political, religious, and theological context.[6] Moreover, we have recognized perhaps for the first time that our

---

1. See Bosch, *Transforming Mission*, 185.
2. Pellegrino, "Future Enters Us."
3. See Bevans, "Migration and Mission," 157–78.
4. A Roman Catholic approach regarding salvation outside the church could be found in *Nostra Aetate*, the Second Vatican Council's Declaration on the Relation of the Church to Non-Christian Religions, proclaimed by his Holiness Pope Paul VI on October 28, 1965.
5. Bevans, "Migration and Mission," 158.
6. Previous to the Second Vatican Council, the *ressourcement* movement of thought in twentieth-century Roman Catholic theology was an appeal to theologians to return to historical sources to inform contemporary understandings. According to the Dominican theologian Yves Congar, the *ressourcement* movement prepared the way for the Council and entails a revival of historical sources. However, *ressourcement* is not merely historical

Understanding of Mission as Prophetic Dialogue

church today is incredibly diverse.[7] No longer can the church's catholicity mean a simple universality nor the church's unity mean a simple uniformity.[8] Christian mission today is in search of new directions to approach our diversity within postmodern and ecumenical paradigms.[9] When talking about mission, we enter into a complexity of ideological, spiritual, and theological understandings which depend on individual perspectives, experience, religious background, and formation and education.

Regardless of the variety and new openness within missiological discourse, there is a common understanding about the need to be sensitive to philosophical, cultural, social, political, spiritual, and contextual movements of the present time, or as the Second Vatican Council puts it, "to read the signs of the times."[10] Therefore, mission is now conceived as a conscious dedication, preparation, and commitment to incarnate the gospel in every culture not only individually but in specific societies. An open attitude (thus, one open to dialogue) must characterize the interior mind-set of the persons undertaking holistically the endeavor of mission.[11]

Nevertheless, along with this new understanding of mission that emerged after the Second Vatican Council, the self-understanding of the church also changed. We can see this reflected in some church documents. Among those from the Second Vatican Council, *Lumen Gentium* (Dogmatic

---

retrieval; it is also critical engagement with the current situation in light of the lesson of the past. It was rather a creative hermeneutical exercise in which the sources of Christian faith were reinterrogated with new questions. With such twentieth-century questions serving as hermeneutical keys, these theologians of *ressourcement* (Hans Urs von Balthasar, Yves Congar, Marie-Dominique Chenu, and Louis Bouyer, to mention some) were able to unlock new areas in the tradition and discover there many of the twentieth-century ideas which neo-scholasticism neglected or even resisted. For these thinkers, doing theology meant doing history. Yet the distinctive approach to historical theology which they shared was neither detached, scholarly reconstruction, nor a futile attempt at what Congar calls "repristination." See Congar, *True and False Reform*, 293–94; Congar, *Holy Spirit*, 150; D'Ambrosio, "Ressourcement Theology," 530–55.

7. See Bevans, "What Has Contextual Theology," 3–4.

8. Dulles, *Catholicity of the Church*, 167. For Robert J. Schreiter, the "new" catholicity between the local and global cultures is a universalizing flow across boundaries that is not totalizing. He presents the catholicity of the church as the dimension that protects and promotes the diversity of culture, worship, and theological formulation, while seeing the interdependence of the global Christian system in the context of an interconnected world. See Schreiter, *New Catholicity*.

9. Scherer and Bevans, *Theological Foundations*, xi–xii.

10. *Gaudium et Spes*, no. 4.

11. See Dorr, *Mission in Today's World*, 193.

Constitution on the Church) emphasized the church and the renewal of its mission in the world. *Lumen Gentium* described the church as the mystical body of Christ and the people of God. Additionally, the theological basis of *Ad Gentes* (Decree on the Church's Missionary Activity) established mission as the very essence of the church's life. As the "universal sacrament of salvation," the church participates in mission in order that "all things can be restored in Christ."[12] Also, *Sacrosanctum Concilium* (Constitution on the Sacred Liturgy) offered liturgical reform, such as the possibility of legitimate variations and adaptations to different cultures for the sake a clearer possibility for evangelization. Moreover, *Nostra Aetate* (Declaration on the Relation of the Church to Non-Christian Religions) recognized that other religions "often reflect a ray of that Truth" and attempted to rethink how to approach non-Christians in ways that were not threatening to them but were engaging them in dialogue and friendship—so anticipating the communion of the reign of God.[13]

Along with this vision of renewal, some regional developments in Latin America and Asia deeply affected the theology of mission of the Catholic Church. In 1968, the Latin American Episcopal Conference met at Medellín, Colombia. There the bishops dealt with the fundamental need to relate the church's life and work to the context of Latin America. They sought to promote social transformation in relation to social justice and liberation from oppressive structures. Medellín provided the stimulus for the development of liberation theology. Similarly, the Hindu-Christian encounter in Sri Lanka and India raised the possibility of *Hindu-Christian* approaches to theology. Raimon Panikkar, a Roman Catholic priest of Hindu and Spanish background, suggested that Christianity and Hinduism both meet in Christ. This encounter was a big step in terms of Christianity relating to other faiths.[14]

Overall, there is a general understanding that mission goes beyond the church. Mission is no longer seen as merely an activity of the church but rather an expression of the very essence of being church. This self-understanding of the church greatly affected the theology of mission: the church was no longer perceived as being *over* the world but rather *sent into* the world and existing for the sake of the world. In this new image,

---

12. *Ad Gentes*, no. 1.

13. *Nostra Aetate*, no. 2. See also Sundermeier, "Theology of Mission," 429–51; and Bevans and Schroeder, *Prophetic Dialogue*, 138–55.

14. See Antes and Waldenfels, "Mission in Non-Christian Religions," 303–7.

Understanding of Mission as Prophetic Dialogue

mission is not an activity of the church but an attribute of God. Mission is seen as the movement of God to the world, and the church is an instrument for that mission.[15]

The following passages offer a glimpse of the understanding of mission that has developed and continues to develop in the twenty-first century.[16]

> The purpose of mission or evangelization is not that every individual should hear of Christ, but that the gospel be incarnated in every culture.[17]

> *Asumir la misión no es encontrarse con una idea, sino con Alguien.*[18]

> Mission has its origin in the heart of God. God is a fountain of sending love. This is the deepest source of mission. It is impossible to penetrate deeper still; there is mission because God loves people.... Our mission has no life of its own: only in the hands of the sending God can it truly be called mission. Not at least since the missionary initiative comes from God alone.[19]

> The mission of the Church is essentially a spiritual activity—the work of the Holy Spirit.... The most important and most desirable ingredient in a person engaged in mission is genuine and deep spirituality.[20]

These passages clearly show how this new understanding of mission is intertwined with the church's new self-understanding.

Having provided the church's understanding of mission as developed since the Second Vatican Council, the next part of this chapter will discuss Bevans's understanding of mission as prophetic dialogue. A brief description of who Stephen Bevans is will introduce this discussion.

---

15. See Bosch, *Transforming Mission*, 399–402.

16. For the chosen definitions of mission, I used the following sources: a synod of bishops, a well-known Hispanic missiologist (Juan Esquedra Bifet), and Catholic and Protestant missiologists (Louis J. Luzbetak is Catholic and David Bosch is Protestant). I am aware that the Asian and African voices are missing, but I wanted to have a voice from my Hispanic background.

17. See Sínodo de los Obispos, "La Nueva Evangelización," no. 5.

18. Esquedra Bifet, *Misionología*, 4. My translation is as follows: "To assume the mission is not encountering an idea, but Someone."

19. Bosch, *Transforming Mission*, 399.

20. Luzbetak, *Church and Cultures*, 1–2.

Toward a New, Praxis-Oriented Missiology

WHO IS STEPHEN B. BEVANS?[21]

Stephen Bevans was born in Baltimore in 1944. Besides his native city, he also grew up in Washington, DC; Riverside, California; and San Diego. He is a Roman Catholic priest in the Society of the Divine Word, a Catholic missionary religious community. He was perpetually professed in 1970 and ordained a priest on September 5, 1971. After doing his theological studies at the Pontifical Gregorian University in Rome, he spent almost nine years as a missionary in the Philippines teaching at a regional diocesan seminary in Northern Luzon. Returning from the Philippines in 1981, he studied to earn a PhD at the University of Notre Dame. His academic training is in systematic theology, and he wrote his doctoral dissertation on the personalistic understanding of God developed in the early twentieth century by the Scots Presbyterian theologian John Wood Oman. Bevans recognizes, however, that his development as a mission theologian is thanks to his dedication as a SVD priest. "I have developed over the years into a mission theologian, and I strongly believe that, were I not an SVD, I would have developed in another direction."[22]

Bevans's work as a missionary in the Philippines deeply impacted his work as a theologian. From this experience, he started developing and deepening his ideas of contextual theology. "Having lived for almost nine years in the Philippines teaching theology at a diocesan seminary in Northern Luzon, and now teaching at Catholic Theological Union in Chicago with its strong mission program and multicultural student body, have shaped the way I have come to understand theology."[23] In 1992, he published one of his main works: *Models of Contextual Theology* (revised and expanded in 2002). Its origins lie in his teaching and theological work when he was a missionary in the Philippines. This was conceived to be more as an exercise in theological method than a work of missiology. "I have become a missiologist, coming in, as it were, through the back door."

The first year after completing his doctorate, while beginning to teach at CTU, he had major leadership roles in societies of missiology. He is currently a faculty member at CTU. He teaches courses on creation, eschatology, and ecclesiology that highlight issues of culture and the church's

---

21. This information was taken mainly from a conversation with Antonio Pernia, SVD, a former SVD Provincial Superior; e-mail exchanges with Stephen Bevans in April 2013 requesting details about his context; and the internet.

22. Stephen Bevans, "Missiology through the Back Door," 367.

23. Bevans, "Missiology through the Back Door," 368.

missionary nature. His work as a theologian of mission has revolved around three themes: context, Trinity, and church.

Bevans is a past president of the American Society of Missiology (2006) and past member of the board of directors of the Catholic Theological Society of America (2007–2009). In March 2012, Bevans was part of the official Vatican delegation to the assembly of the Commission on World Mission and Evangelism in Manila. He has taught and lectured in the United Kingdom, Australia, New Zealand, Mexico, Italy, Ireland, Taiwan, Ghana, Thailand, and Hong Kong.[24] In 2013, the Vatican appointed him as one of three Catholic members of the World Council of Churches' Commission on World Mission and Evangelism. Bevans is presently one of the most influential missiologists and is wholeheartedly dedicated to the works of mission. His categories for describing mission today are used in the sections that follow.

MISSION AS PROPHETIC DIALOGUE

The concept of mission as prophetic dialogue has become very important for my own dedication and work as a missionary religious sister and also in mission studies. In the following pages, I hope to do justice to the richness that this new understanding of mission as dialogue offers us. As mentioned before, Bevans and Schroeder introduced the concept of prophetic dialogue; however, Bevans has developed it further in his own individual work.

Bevans and Schroeder express that there are three strains of theological thought that had characterized mission theology in the late twentieth century from a Roman Catholic perspective. The first strain addresses the church's mission as participation in the life and mission of the Triune God. This perspective can be seen particularly promoted in *Ad Gentes*. The second perspective speaks of mission as establishing God's reign among human beings and within all creation. This is expressed in Paul VI's apostolic exhortation *Evangelii Nuntiandi*. In the third perspective, the church's mission emphasizes the centrality of Christ and the importance of sharing God's truth to all people. This can be seen in John Paul II's encyclical *Redemptoris Missio*.[25] Bevans and Schroeder developed the perspective of mission as *prophetic dialogue*, which attempts to capture the truth of each of the three strains mentioned. This section will develop this perspective

---

24. "Stephen Bevans, S.V.D." Catholic Theological Union, accessed September 11, 2017, http://www.ctu.edu/academics/stephen-bevans-svd.

25. Bevans and Schroeder, *Constants in Context*, 283–84.

Toward a New, Praxis-Oriented Missiology

and introduce how the concept of prophetic dialogue was developed and the resonance the term has in Catholic magisterial documents.

Indian missiologist Michael Amalados used the term prophetic dialogue in 1992. "Religion is called to enter into a prophetic dialogue with the world."[26] For him, mission as prophetic dialogue will help us to be a countercultural presence in a secular world. "Mission is not something added on or exterior to the process of dialogue, but that dialogue itself becomes mission when it moves on from mutual understanding, appreciation, and collaboration to *mutual change*. . . . I can say prophecy is not just another image of mission but the meaning of mission itself."[27]

Then, prophetic dialogue emerged more clearly among the members of SVD, to which Bevans and Schroeder belong, during their General Chapter in the year 2000.[28] As quoted in the introduction but worth repeating, Bevans and Schroeder describe prophetic dialogue in the following way:

> Mission is dialogue. It takes people where they are; it is open to their traditions and culture and experience; it recognizes the validity of their own religious existence and the integrity of their own religious ends. But it is *prophetic* dialogue because it calls people beyond; it calls people to conversion; it calls people to deeper and fuller truth that can only be found in communion with dialogue's Trinitarian ground.[29]

In other words, prophetic dialogue not only encounters the other where they are in their cultural context and religious experience but also helps discern a way forward, a call to go beyond. The approach is not one of imposing doctrine but rather an invitation to go beyond and to spark a transformative process from where people are.

Prophetic dialogue describes missionary thinking and practice that it is not meant to be exclusively Roman Catholic. Bevans proposed prophetic dialogue as a way to think about and practice mission in all Christian traditions.[30] In 2017, I attended the American Society Missiology Conference and had a conversation with a fellow doctoral student who was an Evangelical using the concept of prophetic dialogue for his dissertation and ministry in his church. Both of us exchanged ideas about the

---

26. Amalados, "Mission as Prophecy," 72.
27. Amalados, "Mission as Prophecy," 70.
28. Bevans and Schroeder, *Prophetic Dialogue*, 59.
29. Bevans and Schroeder, *Constants in Context*, 285.
30. See Bevans, "Prophetic Dialogue Approach," 5.

Understanding of Mission as Prophetic Dialogue

application of prophetic dialogue in our respective religious traditions. It was an eye-opening conversation; besides that, the broad approach of mission as prophetic dialogue was clear to me. Nevertheless, the concept has a Roman Catholic shape to it.

> The Roman Catholic emphasis on sacramentality and the fundamental goodness of creation affirmed by the incarnation is evidenced by the insistence that mission today can only be done in dialogue. Dialogue is the foundation of mission. In addition, Catholicism's "both-and" character is reflected in the fact that *both* dialogue *and* prophecy are necessary components of missionary thinking and practice.[31]

God's deepest identity is relationship and communion, a communion that brings healing and wholeness to all creation. A society structured in participation by all, at all levels of social life, recognizes human dignity and creates the maximum opportunity for everyone. This communion in dialogue is the expression of the Trinity.[32] Although prophetic dialogue is not an official term found in Catholic documents, it finds resonance in official Catholic magisterial documents. As an example, in a more recent church document, the apostolic exhortation *Evangelii Gaudium* of Pope Francis to the bishops, clergy, consecrated persons, and the lay faithful on the proclamation of the gospel in today's world, the pope writes, "Evangelization also involves the path of dialogue."[33] When referring to interreligious and ecumenical dialogue, he writes,

> In this dialogue, ever friendly and sincere, attention must always be paid to the essential bond between dialogue and proclamation, which leads the Church to maintain and intensify her relationship with non-Christians. . . . True openness involves remaining steadfast in one's deepest convictions, clear and joyful in one's own identity, while at the same time being "open to understanding those of the other party" and "knowing that dialogue can enrich each side." What is not helpful is a diplomatic openness which says "yes" to everything in order to avoid problems, for this would be a way of deceiving others and denying them the good which we have been given to share generously with others. Evangelization

---

31. Bevans, "Prophetic Dialogue Approach," 5.
32. See Boff, *Trinity and Society*, 11.
33. *Evangelii Gaudium*, no. 238.

Toward a New, Praxis-Oriented Missiology

and interreligious dialogue, far from being opposed, mutually support and nourish one another.[34]

Francis clearly captures the term of prophetic dialogue. Dialogue and prophecy contain a rich dynamic that cannot be separated. These two ideas bring a creative tension. To say mission must be done in prophetic dialogue is to say that

> mission must first and foremost be done with openness and respect for the other, recognizing that God was present before our arrival, that the Spirit has sown the seeds of the word among all peoples and all cultures, and that we missionaries need to be evangelized by those whom we evangelize. However, we do have something to say, and we speak, like the prophets of the Old Testament, not in our own name, but in God's.[35]

Bevans offers a closer look at the inner dynamic of prophetic dialogue. The next section will look at Bevans's understanding of mission as dialogue and his understanding of mission as prophecy.

MISSION AS DIALOGUE

For Bevans, dialogue is more than a practice. It "is more of an attitude, a *habitus*, or spiritual discipline than anything else."[36] It is indeed a kind of spirituality that underlines every aspect of mission. It requires developing a heart "to cultivate the skills and attitudes of deep listening, of 'docility' or the ability to learn from those with whom we work, of respect and word of vulnerability."[37] When referring to dialogue as spirituality, Bevans emphasizes the sense of contemplation that enables the minister or missionary to perceive a particular context in a new way. The spirituality dimension in dialogue was explicitly expressed in the Pontifical Council for Interreligious Dialogue:

> In actual fact the way of fulfilling the Church's mission depends upon the particular circumstances of each local Church, of each Christian. It always implies a certain sensitivity to the social, cultural, religious and political aspects of the situation, as also attentiveness to the "signs of the times" through which the spirit of God

---

34. *Evangelii Gaudium*, no. 251.
35. Bevans and Schroeder, "'We Were Gentle among You,'" 16.
36. Bevans, "Contextual Theology and Prophetic Dialogue," 229.
37. Bevans, "Contextual Theology and Prophetic Dialogue," 229.

is speaking, teaching and guiding. Such sensitivity and attentiveness is developed through a spirituality of dialogue.[38]

The document *Dialogue and Proclamation* quoted above not only makes explicit the spirituality dimension in dialogue but also represents the church's openness and reverence for other religions, recognizing the presence and goodness of God in various cultures. However, when speaking of mission as dialogue, Bevans is introducing a more conscious way of imagining mission. He is not portraying mission as a way of conquering the world for Christ. Rather, he approaches mission with bare feet. Nevertheless, when spirituality of dialogue is used, the sensitivity and attentiveness that are developed lead to the recognition that "mission should be done in vulnerability and in humility, with a sense of being open to be evangelized by those we are evangelizing."[39] Mission as dialogue, then, allows one to encounter the other where they are, respecting the uniqueness of every person, culture, church, and society, and recognizing that the presence of God and the Spirit is already there.

> [Dialogue] allows each party to discover the truth of the other in a process that Doug McConnell, in the article that called for these short reflections, called a "truth encounter." It should be an occasion for each person in the process to wonder at the richness of God's grace and the beauty of that grace as it appears in various cultural traditions. It should lead to God's praise for the Spirit's active presence in the world.[40]

Bevans also emphasizes that dialogue is the nature of God. "God's and Jesus's method was one of dialogue."[41] Jesus is remembered as a man of dialogue, open to all (Jewish, non-Jewish, poor, rich, men, women, children, sick, outcast, and excluded), working for communion because God is communion. Therefore, dialogue is the *how* of mission and in many ways the *what* of mission as well, because it is a sacrament of the way God is.[42] What missiologists have recognized in the last several decades is that if God's inner nature of dialogue and communion is the same as God's outer movement of acting in dialogue and calling to communion, then the very

---

38. See Pontifical Council for Inter-Religious Dialogue, "Dialogue and Proclamation," 78.
39. Bevans and Schroeder, *Prophetic Dialogue*, 22.
40. Bevans, "Interfaith Engagement," 14.
41. Bevans and Schroeder, *Prophetic Dialogue*, 25.
42. Bevans and Schroeder, *Prophetic Dialogue*, 38.

Toward a New, Praxis-Oriented Missiology

nature of God is missionary; God in God's deepest triune nature is communion in mission.[43]

Bevans describes an understanding and imagining of mission as a genuine and deep encounter and acknowledges people as genuine "others." Mission today needs to be carried out in the spirit and practice of dialogue. "Mission is not just a matter of doing things for people. It is first of all a matter of being with people, of listening and sharing with them."[44]

However, mission as dialogue is not an exclusive term developed by Bevans. Understanding of mission as dialogue is foundational to the nature of the church. In fact, the Federation of Asian Bishops' Conferences, indeed the entire church in Asia, is contributing greatly to the global church. We can say that dialogue summarizes the attitude of the Asian church, its mode of evangelization, and its understanding of mission.[45] Dialogue with the poor, with particular contexts, with other religions or philosophies, ideologies, or secular value systems is essential for mission in Asia. In addition, this attitude of dialogue is extended to the way the church witnesses to and proclaims the gospel message and even how it celebrates its liturgy and practices, prayer and contemplation.[46]

In summary, mission as dialogue encompasses respect, openness, willingness to learn, attentiveness, vulnerability, hospitality, humility, and honesty, and it leads us to perceive a *particular context* in a new way.

MISSION AS PROPHECY

For Bevans, an attitude of dialogue is foundational for missionary thinking and practice today. However, without the spirit of prophecy, it lacks direction or purpose.[47] Prophecy, like mission itself, is a complex real-

---

43. For Karl Rahner, there is an identity between the *economic Trinity* (God's outer movement) and the *immanent Trinity* (God's inner nature). The God who is with us, active on our behalf in salvation history, is who God is. It is not the immanent Trinity who is first revealed but the economic Trinity. See Rahner, *Trinity*, 99–102.

44. Dorr, *Mission in Today's World*, 16.

45. See Rosales and Arevalo, *FABC Documents*, 356. The entire volume presents FABC documents covering two decades since FABC was inaugurated by Pope Paul VI in 1970 in Manila and concludes with the plenary assembly in Bandung, Indonesia, in 1990. These documents are an essential source and wellspring for comprehending the dynamic development of mission, theology, church, dialogue, and evangelization in Asia's local churches.

46. Bevans and Schroeder, "'We were Gentle among You,'" 8.

47. Bevans, "Prophetic Dialogue Approach," 7.

ity because of the different aspects interwoven in this action. Moreover, prophecy is accomplished through words and through deeds. It is also a nonverbal and incarnated activity in the witness of an individual, community, or institution.

Dialogue and prophecy are interwoven in the church's missionary work. Bevans depicts three aspects of the nature of prophecy. First, being a prophet means to be someone who dialogues, who listens, who is attentive, who sees, who has sensitivity to peoples and to the world. A prophet listens carefully to God and is able to discern the signs of the times. Second, the root word of prophet in Greek is *pro ephein*, someone who speaks forth. So prophets, after listening and discerning the Word of God, then announce a message, either in words or in deeds. Thus, when prophets speak forth, they offer comfort and hope in times of persecution or despair, set out a vision for the future of what God has for God's people in God's salvific plan, and denounce every form of injustice and oppression.[48] Lastly, prophets speak out in God's name. The prophecy that is delivered is never the prophet's own but God's. Prophets undertake prophetic action aware of their own weakness or limitation but are faithful to the task even to the point of persecution and death. Prophecy, then, entails deep listening to both context and gospel, a humble proclamation of the good news of the gospel with profound openness, presence, and respect for the other and an authentic witnessing as individual, community, or institution.[49]

In Christian understanding, mission is ultimately about sharing the good news of God's reign already inaugurated in the life, death, and resurrection of Jesus of Nazareth. The way the church communicates this good news is through the practice of prophecy. However, Bevans insists that prophecy, in its specific verbal proclamatory form, must always employ a "dialogue method."[50] The church's listening and proclaiming is not a mechanical transmitter of a message, but it is to become what it proclaims. The church's awareness of being still on the way not only keeps the church humble but also challenges its solidarity with the poor and the suffering in

---

48. Bevans, "Prophetic Dialogue Approach," 9.

49. Bevans and Schroeder, *Prophetic Dialogue*, 42–43.

50. "Dialogue method" is a term used by Archbishop Marcello Zago. Bevans borrows his words. See Bevans, "Prophetic Dialogue Approach," 7. For more information, see Marcello Zago, "New Millennium," 5–18.

Toward a New, Praxis-Oriented Missiology

the context of a conflict with the rich and powerful though integrating itself in the paschal mystery of Christ.[51]

In the section "Mission as Dialogue," it was mentioned how the church of Asia has been a great contribution to the entire church by their understanding of mission as dialogue. Similarly, the church of Latin America has been a great contribution to the entire church in their understanding of mission as prophecy.

Liberation theology was inspired by the Second Vatican Council and the papal encyclical *Populorum Progressio*, which Pope Paul VI wrote in 1967 to place the social question in its world-wide context.[52] He emphasized the right for justice in the poorer nations through the aid of the wealthier nations and recognized the social dimension of poverty.[53] Liberation theology emerged in Latin America, though there have been parallel developments in other parts of the world in which experiences of oppression, vulnerability, or marginalization have led to a sustained reflection on the Christian tradition and the reason for mission. The Third World settings of abject poverty and dire human needs have given liberation theology a particular urgency and distinctive outline. The agenda is distinctive in its emphasis on the dialogue between the Christian tradition, social theory, and the insight of the poor and marginalized into their situation, leading to action for change.[54]

It is in the line of "action for change" that liberation theology has greatly impacted the understanding of mission. Liberation theologians like Gustavo Gutierrez, Leonardo Boff, and Jon Sobrino have highlighted the prophetic element of the gospel. For Gutierrez, the ultimate reason for a commitment to the poor and the oppressed does not come by the social analysis we could apply, neither in our human compassion nor in the direct experience of poverty we could have. As Christians, this commitment is based on the God of our faith. It is a prophetic and theocentric option we make.[55]

In summary, those who announce and denounce the social structures of injustice and who are permanently committed to a radical process of transforming the world are acting in a prophetic manner. Mission cannot be reduced to conversion efforts. It includes committing oneself to issues

---

51. Amalados, "Mission as Prophecy," 68.
52. See Boff and Boff, *Introducing Liberation Theology*, 66–67.
53. O'Brien and Shannon, *Catholic Social Thought*, 238.
54. Rowland, *Cambridge Companion to Liberation Theology*, 1–16.
55. Gutiérrez, "Option for the Poor," 181.

of justice, peace, and the integrity of creation, proceeding with cultural and contextual sensitivity. It also needs to proclaim Christian convictions within the context of an honest dialogue with the world's religions.[56]

CONTEXTUAL THEOLOGY AND PROPHETIC DIALOGUE

Bevans says that "contextual theology is an exercise of prophetic dialogue." He also says that "prophetic dialogue is an exercise of contextual theology."[57] Bevans is proposing that the practice of prophetic dialogue and the doing of theology is deeply rooted in a particular context. Contextualization is at the heart of what it means to do theology. Thus, the reason for doing theology contextually is so that the gospel, transmitted in scripture and tradition, can be understood as clearly as possible. Therefore, the goal of contextual theology is prophecy, and doing theology contextually is an exercise of prophetic dialogue.[58]

Contextual theology has become a part of theological vocabulary and is indispensable to the theological enterprise. Nowadays, there is a strong conviction among theologians that the expression of faith has to be done in terms of contemporary society, history, and culture. More attention is now paid to how those circumstances shape the response to the gospel. We hear terms like localization, contextualization, indigenization, and inculturation of theology. "These terms point to the need for and responsibility of Christians to make their response to the gospel as concrete and lively as possible."[59] The need for contextualization arises not from theoretical imperatives but from practical ones. For example, "How was one to celebrate the Eucharist in countries that were Muslim theocracies and forbade the production or importation of fermented beverages?" "How was one to celebrate baptism among the Masai in East Africa, where to pour water on the head of a woman was to curse her with infertility?" "How was one to understand church-state conflict in the repressive regimes of parts of Latin America, where the church was not a power equal to the state, but was now a church for the poor?"[60]

Robert Schreiter points out that Third World churches have recognized the oppressive nature of Western theology that intended to support the

---

56. Bevans, "Theology of Mission," 102.
57. Schreiter, *Constructing Local Theologies*, 2.
58. Bevans, "Contextual Theology and Prophetic Dialogue," 229.
59. Schreiter, *Constructing Local Theologies*, 1.
60. Schreiter, *Constructing Local Theologies*, 2.

Toward a New, Praxis-Oriented Missiology

powerful and the rich.[61] The Western form was normative, and non-Western cultures were considered inferior. Furthermore, Third World churches are becoming aware that one does not have to be educated in the West to be a theologian. The need for Third World churches to adapt and contextualize the gospel to their very specific realities and unique circumstances make contextual theology an imperative. It is clear, moreover, that the need for contextualization is not simply one found amid Third World problems. Contextual theology has cast new light on old ecclesiological and theological problems which have beset the church since modern times.[62]

One of the most important contributions of Bevans to theology has been his book *Models of Contextual Theology*. Drawing on his rich experience as a missionary in the Philippines and his work as a professor at CTU, Bevans provides an exploration of a variety of theologies representing Western and Third World theologians. He proposes six models of contextual theology. The *translational* model takes into account experience, culture, social location, and social change with emphasis on fidelity to the essential content of scripture and tradition. The *anthropological* model is the most radical. This emphasizes cultural identity and its relevance beyond scripture and tradition alone. The *praxis* model focuses on the identity of Christians within a particular context as understood in terms of social change. The *synthetic* model is midway between context (experience, culture, social location, social change) and scripture and tradition, relying on scriptural justification. The *transcendental* model focuses not only on the content but the subject who is articulating and enabling the expression of one's faith in an authentically contextual manner. The *countercultural* model, which Bevans considers more conservative, recognizes the importance of context but does not trust its sanctity and relational power. This one emphasizes the disjunctions between culture and revelation and gives radical priority to gospel proclamation. Each of the models invites us to enter into a creative dialogue, and each model responds to a specific situation.[63]

Contextual theology, then, includes a dialogue between the experience preserved in scripture and tradition and the experience of the present

---

61. I realize that the expression "Third World" is increasingly being criticized for its stratification, as the phrase "Global South" becomes more common. In this research, however, as it has appeared so often in these publications, I render its use.

62. Bevans, "Models of Contextual Theology," 185–202.

63. See Bevans, *Models of Contextual Theology*.

particular context, such as specific cultures, women and men of diverse social locations, other Christians in mission, and people of other religions:

> We can say, then, that doing theology contextually means doing theology in a way that takes into account two things. First, it takes into account the faith experience of the *past* that is recorded in scriptures and kept alive, preserved, defended—and perhaps even neglected or suppressed—in tradition.... Second, contextual theology takes into account the experience of the present, the *context*.[64]

Since prophetic dialogue is practiced in a dialectic of openness to the new and fidelity to scripture and tradition, "contextual theology is done with the same dialogical openness, prophetic fidelity and creativity."[65] Moreover, both prophetic dialogue and contextual theology require deep listening to the gospel, to the people, and to a specific context. In other words, "what makes contextual theology contextual is the recognition of the validity of another *locus theologicus*: present human experience. Theology that is contextual realizes that culture, history, contemporary thought forms . . . are to be considered, along with scripture and tradition, as valid sources for theological expression."[66]

When doing mission in prophetic dialogue, one needs to be contextual. The way we witness to the gospel in mission will depend on the situation we find ourselves:

> When does one need to be prophetic in participating in God's mission? When does one need to be dialogical? It is in discerning the answers to these questions that one needs to think contextually. In our twenty-first century global, multicultural, minority, poor, and vulnerable church, the way we live our Christian lives and witness to the gospel in mission will very much depend on the situation in which we find ourselves.[67]

Darrell Whiteman, an anthropologist and missiologist, sees three functions of contextualization. The first function is "to communicate the Gospel in word and deed and to establish the church in ways that make sense to people within their local cultural context, presenting Christianity in such a way that it meets people's deepest needs and penetrates their

---

64. Bevans, *Models of Contextual Theology*, 5.
65. Bevans, "Contextual Theology and Prophetic Dialogue," 227.
66. See Bevans, *Models of Contextual Theology*, 4.
67. Bevans, "Theology of Mission," 107.

Toward a New, Praxis-Oriented Missiology

worldview, thus allowing them to follow Christ and remain within their own culture."[68] The gospel does not take people out of their culture but calls them to be full participants in it.[69] Sadly, the mission of the church often required people to abandon their cultures. However, postcolonial hermeneutics have helped us to see how our understanding and practice of faith has been shaped by our own culture and context. We often assumed that our culturally conditioned interpretation of the gospel was the gospel. "Contextualization is a fine balancing act between necessary involvement in the culture, being in the situation, and also maintaining an outside, critical perspective that is also needed."[70]

The second function of contextualization is "to offend—but only for the right reasons, not the wrong ones."[71] When the gospel is presented in word and deed and the fellowship of believers is organized along appropriate cultural forms, then people will more likely be confronted with the "offense" of the gospel, exposing oppressive structures and unhealthy behavior patterns within their culture. Contextualization becomes prophetic as it challenges the context through gospel values.

The third function of contextualization in mission is "to develop contextualized expressions of the Gospel so that the Gospel itself will be understood in ways the universal church has neither experienced nor understood before, thus expanding our understanding of the kingdom of God."[72] For Whiteman, contextualization is a form of mission in reverse: one can learn from other cultures on how to be more Christian in one's own context. This connects the particular with the universal because contextualization enlarges our view of God as the God of all peoples. God can no longer simply be the god of myself, my family, my community, my nation but the God of all.[73]

For Bevans, contextual theology is born out of dialogue, and dialogue is required for the three functions of contextualization mentioned above. This dialogical character bears witness to the fact that Christianity is not a religious way that calls women and men out of their context. Rather, it is an invitation to discover the Spirit's presence in movements, persons,

---

68. Whiteman, "Contextualization," 2–7.
69. Bevans, "Contextual Theology and Prophetic Dialogue," 230.
70. Whiteman, "Contextualization," 3.
71. Whiteman, "Contextualization," 3.
72. Whiteman, "Contextualization," 4.
73. Whiteman, "Contextualization," 4.

human experience, cultures, and history. Contextual theologizing is indeed a practice of prophetic dialogue.[74]

In summary, contextual theologies can provide new agendas, new methods, new voices, and a new dialogue.[75] Therefore, missiology is more than a discipline concerned with "the missions" but is a way of thinking about church and theology that just might inspire Christianity with new life.[76]

EXERCISING PROPHETIC DIALOGUE

In this section, I will present a personal ministerial experience that embodies the concept of prophetic dialogue. I will refer to this example throughout the other chapters to illustrate and indicate the importance and intertwined elements in the work of Bevans and Paulo Freire.

I am a religious Catholic missionary sister from the Verbum Dei community. I have been working for many years with the immigrant Latino population in California. For eight years, I lived and carried out my ministry in Long Beach, California. It was the Easter of 2008 and the pastor of St. Anthony's church, the parish where my community is located, asked me if we could organize a service on Good Friday. This service was to be dedicated to all those who, due to their legal situation, were unable to be present at the funeral of their loved ones who passed away in their native country. Many of our immigrants carry a heavy burden of not being able to say goodbye, to forgive, or simply to express feelings to their family members that have passed away. Due to their legal situation, immigrants experience a great deal of vulnerability and anger.

The Good Friday service happened to occur within a specific political moment and in a unique personal situation. At that time, there were several *redadas* (federal raids) in the Los Angeles area. People were afraid of being visited by Immigration and Customs Enforcement (ICE) at their workplace and being sent back to their countries of origin without having the chance to notify their families. *Las redadas* were causing a lot of fear and anxiety in our people. Simultaneously, the pastor and I had both lost our parents the year before and were still dealing with our own grief. We were both very vulnerable like our people. We did not have all the answers to pain and suffering, and we were trying to make sense of faith when in pain.

---

74. Bevans, "Contextual Theology and Prophetic Dialogue," 232.
75. Bevans, "Theology of Mission," 101.
76. Bevans, "Theology of Mission," 200.

Toward a New, Praxis-Oriented Missiology

The service began listening to the Word of God followed by a short homily encompassing eschatological hope. The people had a moment of silence to reconnect with their unsolved feelings. Using Taizé songs, we venerated the cross. Instead of a penitential rite or confession, each person shared their unfinished closures with the pastor in an ambience of silence. After being heard, they kissed the cross and continued to surround the cross with the certainty that Jesus had kissed their pain. It was indeed a powerful healing service. That Good Friday, St. Anthony's church was holding the tears of a large group of undocumented immigrants.

Bevans says, *doing contextual theology is an exercise of prophetic dialogue and prophetic dialogue is an exercise of contextual theology*. Also, *what makes contextual theology contextual is the recognition of the validity of the present human experience*. When one is placed in ministerial situations, theology is born out of human experiences. In retrospect, I discovered a profound insight for me held within this experience, but in the moment, it was quite challenging. To listen, to be open, to be a vulnerable, constant learner is not an easy task. Bevans reminds us that the first step in doing theology and doing mission is discernment born out of deep listening to both context and gospel.

A simple Good Friday service became an intentional exercise of prophetic dialogue. Using Bevans's words, *prophetic dialogue is more of an attitude, habitus, or spiritual discipline, than anything else*. We need to approach mission with profound openness, presence, and respect for the other. The exercise of prophetic dialogue led me and the pastor to listen to the fear that the political context was creating in our immigrant people due to *las redadas*. It also led us to listen to and acknowledge the human experience that the pastor and I encountered. We were grieving the death of our own parents. Every week as ministers, we hear many cases from people losing family members and not being able to visit them due to their legal situation. My attitude and openness to the grief of our people is now different. The personal and social context of Easter 2008 made me face new questions that needed new answers about God, faith, and eschatological hope. Sadly, sometimes mission can become a question of being practical. The mutual learning process is ignored and is mysteriously the most enriching.

After the service, some parishioners asked the pastor to add the service as a Good Friday program for immigrants. It is impossible to simply repeat an activity if there is an exercise of deep listening to the context and the gospel. The following year, we needed to offer a different service focused on the children of the immigrant population. We had the challenge of continuing to exercise prophetic dialogue and understand mission as a transformative process *in* and *from* the specific context.

Having looked at the concept of prophetic dialogue embodied in a ministerial experience, this section focused on the richness that prophetic dialogue has to offer to the church when being intentional in its practice. In this way, prophetic dialogue allows us to encounter the other in their cultural and historical context, engaging critically with the Christian tradition and discerning a call to transformation.

WHAT DOES PROPHETIC DIALOGUE HAVE TO OFFER TO THE TWENTY-FIRST-CENTURY CHURCH?

This section will first offer an overview of some of the main challenges that the Christian church of the twenty-first century is presently facing. Then, it will present what prophetic dialogue has to offer to the twenty-first-century church.

In *Transforming Mission*, David Bosch points out some factors that are reshaping the Christian church, theology, and mission. (1) The worldwide process of secularization and the advance of science and technology offer us ways and means of dealing with the demands of modern life, which have made faith in God nuanced. (2) The West is slowly but steadily being dechristianized.[77] Atheism, unbelief, superstition, and secularism are more common. (3) Because of the increasing migration of people of many faiths, we now live in a pluralistic religious world. Freedom of religion and greater awareness of other faiths force Christians to reevaluate their attitudes toward other faiths. (4) The rich are getting richer and the poor poorer. The structures of oppression and exploitation are being challenged as never before. (5) For centuries, the practices of Western theology and Western ecclesiology were normative and undisputed. Societies now seek their own local cultural identities. Third World theologies, like liberation theology, African theology, Asian theology, indigenous theology, feminist theology, to mention only some, are giving voice to minority groups. These theologies have also contributed profound uncertainties in Western churches and mission because of the challenge to Eurocentric, patriarchal, de-historicized assumptions about theological construction. (6) People are

---

77. David B. Barrett, George T. Kurian, and Todd M. Johnson calculated that in Europe and North America an average of 53,000 people are leaving the Christian church from one Sunday to the next. See Barrett et al., *World by Countries*, 9.

becoming aware of our capacity to destroy the earth and make it uninhabitable for future generations.[78] Other factors can be added to this list, but it is precisely in this new paradigm and new direction that Christian church, theology, and mission are bearing new thought and practice. It is our challenge to respond imaginatively to paradigm changes.[79]

Taking into account the previous factors, what does prophetic dialogue have to offer to the twenty-first-century church? To answer this question, I will use the insights that Bevans gave in the opening keynote address at the Contextual Theology Conference held at United Theological College in Sydney, Australia, in April 2009. Before proceeding to answer the question, I would like to emphasize that Bevans's understanding of prophetic dialogue is not separate from contextual theology: *prophetic dialogue is an exercise of contextual theology*. In my concluding remarks, I will make more explicit the intertwined relationship of these two concepts.

New Agenda

What prophetic dialogue and contextual theology offer to the church of the twenty-first century is a *new agenda*. The practice of prophetic dialogue offers deep listening to the context and the human experience. Context not only shapes the content and method of our theologizing and doing mission but also determines the questions we ask and highlights the things that are important.[80] The factors mentioned above bring new questions and require not only new answers but also new ways of understanding the classic questions about God, church, creation, anthropology, and eschatology, to mention some. For example, in his post-synodal apostolic exhortation *Amoris Laetitia* to bishops, priests and deacons, consecrated persons, Christian married couples, and all the lay faithful on love in the family, Pope Francis offers a new agenda to the church's teaching on marriage and family and extends an invitation to Christian families to value the gifts of marriage and family amid postmodern challenges and the

---

78. See Bosch, *Transforming Mission*, 3–4, 188–89; and Scherer and Bevans, *Basic Statements*, ix.

79. Bosch speaks of five historical paradigms according to which missionary activity has been carried out in the past. However, he proposes that a postmodern and ecumenical paradigm is emerging as a result of what is happening in our time and in our world. Christian mission today is faced with issues that invite the church to grow and respond in directions that were unthinkable in the past. Therefore, Bosch concludes that mission today needs to be carried out in "bold humility." Bosch, *Transforming Mission*, 489.

80. Bevans, "What Has Contextual Theology," 12.

different social contexts of the twenty-first century. The deep listening to the "signs of the times" offers new agendas.

New Method

Prophetic dialogue offers the church of the twenty-first century a *new method*. The exercise of prophetic dialogue and contextual theology takes experience seriously, and the dialogue between the human experience, tradition, and context can bring endless creative methods for probing experience in the light of faith. As mentioned earlier, mission as dialogue allows us to encounter the other where they are, respecting the uniqueness of every culture, church, and society and recognizing the presence of God and the Spirit already present. *The* new method does not exist. Prophetic dialogue is more of a spirituality than a strategy. To listen, to be open, to be vulnerable, and to be a constant learner are not granted by applying a strategy. However, the practice of transformative action in specific situations arise in the measure by which we listen to the Spirit and the gospel, the tradition, the particular cultures, and the needs of that culture. For example, working with a group of indigenous women in Latin America, a group of women in a small tribe of Cameroon, or a group of aboriginal women in Australia is not the same. One can be familiar with indigenous theology, but the approach and method for every ethnic group will be broadly different. The creativity for method and the actualization of theology and mission depend on deep listening.

New Voices

Prophetic dialogue can open our ears to *new voices*. It was mentioned that Third World theologies—liberation theology, African theology, Asian theology, and indigenous theology—are giving voice to minority groups. Giving voice is one of the main tasks of prophetic dialogue and contextual theology. It is a gift that prophetic dialogue offers to the church of the twenty-first century: new voices.

New Dialogue

Prophetic dialogue offers the church of the twenty-first century a *new dialogue*. Prophetic dialogue is the access to do theology and ministry that is contextual. Both prophetic dialogue and contextual theology are rooted in its own context and honor one's own context and experience. This way

Toward a New, Praxis-Oriented Missiology

of doing theology and mission has been necessary and crucial to face the challenges that twenty-first-century theological thinking is experiencing. One can see that initiating a dialogue with different contexts already offers a new dialogue. However, this new dialogue requires a step forward. Aside from our own particular contexts, there is another context for exercising prophetic dialogue and doing theology in the church of this century: the global context. Therefore, this new dialogue needs to take into account the global context as well. Prophetic dialogue does not intend to be enclosed within specific contexts. However, this can also be its pitfall. A new dialogue in a global context will help to deepen one's own insights and will allow to perceive similarities between very different cultures or social locations. Additionally, dialogue in a global context can challenge and enrich one's understanding. The dynamism that is intrinsic to dialogue—enlightening, stretching, and enriching—is necessary for both the particular and the global context. Therefore, prophetic dialogue offers the church today a new dialogue in particular contexts and in the global context.

CONCLUDING THOUGHTS

The understanding of missionary thinking and practice suggested by the term prophetic dialogue is indeed grounded in the *missio Dei* and is based on the principle of mutual enrichment and exchange. Prophetic dialogue foresees the need for a process of transformation and conversion of perspectives and attitudes. This fundamental point of convergence occurs not only in the head but primarily in the heart. Therefore, the persistence of Bevans about prophetic dialogue being more of a spirituality than a strategy is justified.[81] And that it is *more of an attitude, habitus, or spiritual discipline* fall into place.

> Mission can be done, in the final analysis by women and men who pray regularly, who spend time in contemplation, who share their faith in theological reflection, who study and read the Bible individually and in community, who steep themselves in the wisdom of Christian tradition, who constantly hone their skills in reading cultures and contexts, and who understand cultural trends and current events.[82]

---

81. See Schreiter, *Ministry of Reconciliation*.
82. Bevans and Ross, *Mission on the Road to Emmaus*, xv.

Understanding of Mission as Prophetic Dialogue

There is the danger of searching for efficacy or good strategies in mission. Prophetic dialogue offers us clearer wisdom that mission is not simply doing. The creativity, initiative, being a constant learner, and being able to offer an adequate response to the different challenges presented in the different contexts in missionary activity are born in the contemplative heart.

To practice mission as prophetic dialogue is not something new and unique in only Bevans's thought and work. We saw how the church's mission after the Second Vatican Council exposes the need to be sensitive to dialogue, on the one hand, and confident in prophetic witness and proclamation, on the other. However, the call of mission to be more intentional is new and different. This is one of the greatest contributions that Bevans's work offers us. Prophetic dialogue is new because it gives new life and new eyes to Christian thinking about theology, mission, and missionary practice by inviting us to constantly listen and to be open to the present context and different cultures. Prophetic dialogue is different because it allows us to critically engage the historical Christian tradition and contemporary understandings of theological resources, norms, and *loci*.

We cannot separate dialogue and prophecy. Mission is dialogical prophecy. As Bevans says, *the question is not, is it one or the other?* Rather, the question is, when should the dialogical aspect in a mission setting be employed, and when should the missionary act or speak prophetically in words and deeds? This is the reason for the importance of openness, listening, and recognizing that the presence of God is already there. Therefore, engaging in *missio Dei* is an art. As Bevans and Schroeder put it in their book *Prophetic Dialogue*, doing mission as prophetic dialogue is joining God in the dance of mission.[83]

Bevans's understanding of contextual theology as prophetic dialogue is unique. First, Bevans suggests that theology should be done in a dialectic of openness and critique, recognizing the validity of present human experience and fidelity to scripture and tradition. This is an important principle because in many cases theology is limited to pure reflexive thinking, leaving the dialogical element outside. Second, Bevans is applying the same spiritual principle applied in prophetic dialogue to theologizing in the twenty-first century. Spirituality is essential for theological discourse. Third, theology and mission cannot be separated, as dialogue and prophecy cannot be separated either. "The work of mission is always grounded in

---

83. Bevans and Schroeder, *Prophetic Dialogue*, 18.

Toward a New, Praxis-Oriented Missiology

a theology."[84] In fact, in the past, the predominant theology was Western theology. Contextual theologizing offers a constant reflection, a constructive critique, and a more applicable theology in the concrete realities of the people and times. "The practice of mission as prophetic dialogue demands constant and thorough contextual theologizing."[85] For Bevans, prophetic dialogue and contextual theology reflect the mission of God, whose Word is found in all human contexts and calls us to truth.

Prophetic dialogue offers us a *new hermeneutic*. Using prophetic dialogue as a hermeneutic to theologizing and to do mission helps us to continually see how our understanding and practice of faith is and has been shaped by our own culture and context. One of the vulnerabilities in theology and mission is that we often assume that our culturally conditioned interpretation of the gospel *is* the gospel. Prophetic dialogue can provide us with tools not only to interpret the context in the light of scripture and tradition but also to offer a new interpretation of the gospel in light of different cultures and contexts. One of the constant challenges of missionary activity and mission methods is the need for constant adaptation and listening to the signs of the times. Therefore, the hermeneutic that prophetic dialogue suggests is keen for a missiological endeavor.

The following chapter will present Paulo Freire and his concept of *conscientização*, applying a biographical approach with the intention of capturing the history, spirit, and legacy of Freire. The hope is that the reader can grasp Freire's development and importance of the concept of *conscientização*, which is historically grounded, and then see its theory and its practice applied in new and potentially productive ways for mission praxis today.

---

84. Bevans, "Contextual Theology and Prophetic Dialogue," 237.
85. Bevans, "Contextual Theology and Prophetic Dialogue," 237.

2

Paulo Freire's Concept of *Conscientização*: A Commitment to Process

Porque amar não é apenas um ato livre, mas um ato para a liberdade.

E amor que não pode produzir mais liberdade, não é amor.[1]

—PAULO FREIRE, "CONSCIENTISATION"

PAULO FREIRE'S EDUCATIONAL WORK can be viewed from a vast number of perspectives. However, the aim of this chapter is not so much to display his educational thought and philosophy as much as to present his concept of *conscientização*. The deep meaning of this word portrays Freire's understanding of education: an exercise in freedom, an act of knowing, and a critical approach to reality. Furthermore, *conscientização* holds theory and practice together as a mutually enriching process.

This chapter will first present who Paulo Freire is and the philosophical influences which caused Freire to approach *conscientização* as a process. Second, it will introduce the concept of *conscientização* and explore why and how Freire arrived at the importance of *conscientização*. Third, it will discuss whether *conscientização* is still relevant today. Finally, the chapter will conclude by showing how *conscientização* leads to hope of transformation.

---

1. My translation is as follows: "For loving is not only a free act, it is an act for freedom. And love that cannot produce more freedom, is not love."

Toward a New, Praxis-Oriented Missiology

WHO IS PAULO FREIRE?

Paulo Freire's revolutionary pedagogy and the development of his educational ideas are truly remarkable. Freire was a tireless educator who struggled for the liberation of the poorest of the poor. His thought evolved from his personal upbringing and from his reflections on the experiences of those with whom he lived and worked.[2]

Paulo Freire was born on September 19, 1921, into a middle-class family in Recife, Brazil. Freire became familiar with poverty and hunger during the Great Depression in the 1930s after his father died. He ended up being two years behind in school, and his social life revolved around playing soccer with other poor children. He learned from them. These experiences shaped his later concerns for the poor and helped construct his educational viewpoint.[3]

Freire had stated that poverty and hunger severely affected his ability to learn. This influenced his decision to dedicate his life to improving the lives of the poor: "I didn't understand anything because of my hunger. I wasn't dumb. It wasn't lack of interest. My social condition didn't allow me to have an education. Experience showed me once again the relationship between social class and knowledge."[4] After his family situation improved, he was able to study law at the University of Recife in 1943. He also studied philosophy in the area of phenomenology and psychology of language.

In 1944, Freire married Elza Maia Costa de Oliveira, a grade school teacher. They had five children and were happily married until Elza's death in 1986. He was professor of history and philosophy of education at the University of Recife until 1964. In the 1960s, he was involved with a popular education movement to deal with massive illiteracy.[5] In 1962, there were widespread experiments in education based on his method, and the movement was extended under the patronage of the federal government. From 1963 to 1964, there were courses on Freire's pedagogy for education coordinators in all Brazilian states, and a plan was drawn up for the establishment of two thousand cultural circles to reach two million adults who were illiterate.

Unfortunately, a military coup in 1964 put an end to that effort. Freire was imprisoned as a traitor for seventy days. In prison, he began his first

---

2. See Freire, *Cartas a Cristina*; Collins, *Paulo Freire: His Life*.
3. Dale and Hyslop-Margison, *Paulo Freire*, 1–5.
4. Gadotti, *Reading Paulo Freire*, 5.
5. Araújo Freire, "Paulo Freire," 1–13.

Paulo Freire's Concept of Conscientização: A Commitment to Process

educational work, *Educação Como Practica da Libertade* (*Education as the Practice of Freedom*). After a brief exile in Bolivia, Freire worked in Chile for five years for the Christian Democratic Agrarian Reform Movement and the Food and Agriculture Organization of the United Nations. While Freire was in exile, he was able to finish and publish his first book *Education as the Practice of Freedom* in 1967.[6] He followed this with his most famous book *Pedagogy of the Oppressed*. In 1969, Freire was offered a visiting professorship at Harvard University in Cambridge, Massachusetts. The following year, *Pedagogy of the Oppressed* was published in both Spanish and English, vastly expanding its reach. However, because of political disputes between Freire, Christian socialists, and successive authoritarian military dictatorships, the book was not published in Brazil until 1974.[7]

After a year at Harvard, Freire moved to Geneva, Switzerland, to work as a roving ambassador of literacy to the Third World of the World Council of Churches, a point which will be mentioned later. During this time, Freire acted as an advisor on education reform in former Portuguese colonies in Africa, particularly Guinea-Bissau and Mozambique.

In 1979, he was allowed to return to Brazil, and he moved back in 1980. Freire joined the Workers' Party in the city of Sao Paulo and acted as a supervisor for its adult literacy project from 1980 to 1986. When the Workers' Party prevailed in the municipal elections in 1988, Freire was appointed Secretary of Education for Sao Paulo. The importance of Freire's ideas come from the vast experience of having been working in various parts of the world and in different contexts, all interwoven with his own life experience. On May 2, 1997, Freire died of heart failure in Sao Paulo.

In order to understand Freire's philosophical influence, the next section will present his sociohistorical context.

FREIRE'S PHILOSOPHICAL INFLUENCE

In the early 1960s, various reform movements flourished in Brazil as socialists, communists, populists, labor leaders, Christian militants, and others sought their own sociopolitical goals. At this time, Brazil had a population of 34.5 million people, of whom only 15.5 million could vote. In Brazil, it was required to write and read in order to vote; illiteracy among the poor

---

6. See Freire, *Education*.

7. This was during the time of General Ernesto Geisel, who was the dictator president that began the process of a slow and controlled political liberalization in Brazil that allowed Freire's work to be published in the country.

served the interests of the dominant minority.[8] During the presidency of João Goulart (1961–1964), a populist leader, there was the rise of peasant leagues and other cultural movements that aimed at consciousness-raising and nationwide literacy campaigns. It was in this context that Freire was appointed as the director of *Departamento de Extensión Cultural de la Universidad de Recife*, which allowed him to apply his theories.

Looking at the history of Brazil, one can see the evolution from colonialism, the struggle of masses against government by a powerful few, to dependence upon foreign capital and foreign economies. The Brazilian government supported and fostered a culture of dependence. Freire witnessed this culture of dependence, which reached and affected not only the economic and political reality but literature, art, religion, and family customs. Therefore, Freire's works and writings are "dominated by the desire to make these humanistic values fully available to everyone. He is consequently critical of both capitalist and communist societies because he believes that neither allows for the maximum self-development and growth in freedom of all men and women."[9]

It is easy to categorize Freire as a humanist. But the above ideas are not restricted to classical humanism. Freire was able to unite observations and reflections from several modern thinkers like Karl Marx, György Lukács, Erich Seligmann Fromm, Antonio Gramsci, Frantz Fanon, Albert Memmi, Jean-Paul Sartre, Karel Kosik, Simone Weil, Agnes Heller, and so many others.[10] Moreover, Freire's thinking flowed from his varied life experiences that led him to articulate political liberation. It is impossible to account for every person who shaped Freire's thought. Nevertheless, five philosophical strains very well ensemble and offer a general understanding of Freire's philosophical influence: (1) personalism, (2) existentialism, (3) phenomenology, (4) Marxism, and (5) Christianity.

Personalism

Personalism is an approach or system of thought which regards the person as the ultimate explanatory, epistemological, ontological, and axiological principle of all reality.[11] This system of thought is an optimistic way

8. Scocuglia, *História das Ideias*, 29–32.
9. Donohue, "Paulo Freire," 168.
10. One can see in Freire's main works, especially in his book *Pedagogy of the Oppressed*, that the quotes and references he used are mainly from these modern thinkers.
11. Williams and Bengtsson, "Personalism."

of looking at the world and a summons to action that certainly stamped Freire's thought. Freire was deeply influenced by Emmanuel Mounier, a French personalist and intellectual prominent in the resistance against Adolf Hitler. Mounier advocated practical policies. He questioned the ability of bourgeois liberalism, with its materialist and individualist roots, to respond to an economic crisis or to satisfy the moral and spiritual aspirations of the human person.[12] For example, the rise of totalitarian ideologies led to the assault of human dignity as Hitler and Stalin destroyed millions of lives. Mounier articulated a clear and accurate defense of the human person and offered a personalist communitarian approach to politics. Mounier saw human beings as free and creative persons, capable of responsible liberty.[13] He defended the unity of the human person as both a material and spiritual being and affirmed human equality as a reality rooted in the dignity of all. He rejected the idea that human beings are nothing but automated machines, programmed to pursue their own selfish interests and lacking authentic free will.[14]

Some of the themes mentioned above are found later in Freire. Other themes in Freire's work include the following: human beings are free and creative persons, history has a meaning, and notwithstanding wars and other disasters, history drives toward liberation. An optimistic way of looking at the world and a summons to action certainly stamped Freire's thought.[15]

Existentialism

In Freire's writings, one can see the names of and quotes from Sartre, Jasper, Marcel, Heidegger, and other existentialist thinkers. The exact influence of each philosopher will not be possible to trace, but it will be worthwhile to depict some basic concepts and values in Freire derived from existentialist philosophy.

Freire's passion for "true acts of knowing," authentic and inauthentic states of existence, freedom for human beings to become subjects, the value of freedom as self-making, the way of questioning the capitalist exploitation and the utilitarianism of the educational system (banking education), and alienation from oneself, to mention some, are existentialist

12. Collins, *Paulo Freire: Filosofía Educativa*, 193.
13. See Mounier, *Personalism*, 9.
14. See Christian, "Enduring Wisdom of Emmanuel Mounier."
15. Collins, *Paulo Freire: Filosofía Educativa*, 194.

concerns. Moreover, existentialists emphasize human beings' freedom to choose and to act.

Freire placed emphasis upon dialogue as an essential tool to help the person become a subject and not an object, a political tool for real democratization. He was mainly influenced by Sartre's existentialism, which is a philosophy of being and existence. Being cannot be understood through purely rational thought; it must be understood through existence and lived experience.[16] Also, a fundamental part of human existence is based on the freedom to make choices.[17] Freire adopted Sartre's idea that the quality of human existence is tied to the choices that human beings make in society and how these choices affect others. Therefore, *conscientização* is, in a way, the realization of one's existential possibilities to act upon the world in morally appropriate ways that respect other's freedom.[18]

Phenomenology

Freire's approach to the analysis of the structures of experience and consciousness came mainly from the influence of Husserl's phenomenological method. Freire adopted the principle that exploration of consciousness is a prerequisite to an accurate knowledge of reality, and it enables the knower to study reality when fully intended upon what appears to the perceiving subject.[19] Moreover, the necessity for reflection upon one's consciousness is essential in Freire's thought and pedagogy. The attention that Freire paid to human states of consciousness have marked him as an idealist or dreamer who seeks to change social reality by a simple change of human consciousness. As mentioned, this criticism is an oversimplification.

Freire uses a phenomenological investigation of reality and consciousness in order to unveil the mode of human knowing.[20] This was important in Freire's method so that students can discover themselves as part of reality, distinct from the reality that the capitalist system placed on them, and capable of examining it. Therefore, consciousness leads to the discovery of the social conditioning of consciousness and the power of thinking subjects to act on their own behalf.[21]

16. Dale and Hyslop-Margison, *Paulo Freire*, 122.
17. See Sartre, "Man Makes Himself."
18. Dale and Hyslop-Margison, *Paulo Freire*, 125.
19. Duarte, "Thinking Together as One," 180–88.
20. Collins, *Paulo Freire: His Life*, 31.
21. Collins, *Paulo Freire: His Life*, 32.

Paulo Freire's Concept of Conscientização: A Commitment to Process

Marxism

Freire was attracted and deeply influenced by the Marxist interpretation of history and culture. For Marx, class struggle was a central element in the analysis of social change. In order to perceive the resonance in Freire with Marxist philosophy, it is important to take into consideration Freire's Third World Latin American background: the contrast he saw and experienced between the rich and the poor, the powerful and powerless, and the injustice due to economics and the unequal distribution of resources. This generated in Freire a dialectical thinking stimulated in an environment where contrasts were painfully evident. Marx's critique of capitalism and his articulation of the fundamental value of freedom and equality cannot be achieved by isolated individuals subject to the laws of the market.[22] Only a collective, social subject can realize these values. All this resonated with Freire's ideals. Furthermore, Freire was also influenced by György Lukács's work *History and Class Consciousness*, which was written around the First World War in the wake of the wave of proletarian rebellion across Europe. Lukács, a Marxist philosopher, elaborated a philosophy of revolution that supplemented Marxist economics.[23] He reinstated the centrality of consciousness as a practical activity and political force.[24] Certainly, Freire was persuaded by Lukács's critique of reification in capitalism and his formulated vision of Marxism as a self-conscious transformation of society.

Christianity

The Christian influence in Freire's thought is obvious. It is known that Freire was born into a Catholic family. Brazil is still one of the largest Catholic nations in the world, so Christianity has been a normalized language in Brazil. Freire withdrew from the practice of Catholicism for several years and returned to it because of the lectures of Alceu Amoroso Lima, known by the pseudonym Tristão de Ataíde. He was a writer, journalist, and activist from Brazil and founder of the Brazilian Christian Democracy. Tristão de Ataíde converted to Catholicism and became a strong opponent of authoritarianism and fascism. He was an advocate for freedom of the press during the period of military dictatorship. During that same period, Freire was

---

22. Feenberg, *Philosophy of Praxis*, 3.
23. Feenberg, *Philosophy of Praxis*, 2.
24. Lukás, "Class Consciousness," 31.

Toward a New, Praxis-Oriented Missiology

becoming familiar with the work of Christian personalists like Mounier (mentioned previously), Jacques Maritain, and Georges Bernanos.[25]

During the Great Depression, Brazil's working class was especially hurt by the economic downturn. Brazil lacked any formal nationalized social support system to help unemployed workers. Many Brazilians turned to the Catholic Church for assistance and hope. The people's experiences of oppression, vulnerability, or marginalization led to a sustained reflection of how these experiences related to the Christian tradition.

In Freire's view, "traditional forms of religion serve to preserve the status quo."[26] Liberation theology was a reaction to that formal religious tradition, and it was a powerful response to poverty through the political activism of Catholic priests.[27] Liberation theology became a central component in Freire to work against corporate domination and social injustice within Latin America, not only Brazil. Liberation theology held many views consistent with Freire's socialist objectives and offered a coherent proclamation of faith in that the gospel values were reflected in the lives of the people committed to social change.[28] It is important to mention that Freire maintained a critical attitude toward those who used religion as a tool of oppression.[29] He also held with certainty that neoliberalism, capitalism, authoritarianism, and consequently social injustice were not God's will.[30]

Having looked at Freire's philosophical influences, which caused him to use *conscientização* as the base of his pedagogical development and work, the next section will focus on understanding what *conscientização* is and its importance for a process of social transformation.

WHAT IS *CONSCIENTIZAÇÃO*?

Conscientização can be defined as the process through which human beings achieve a deepened awareness of both the sociocultural reality that shapes their lives and their capacity to transform that reality.[31] It involves praxis, understood as the dialectic relationship of action and reflection.[32] Freire

25. Collins, *Paulo Freire: Filosofía Educativa*, 5–6.
26. Mayo, *Gramsci, Freire and Adult Education*, 61.
27. Dale and Hyslop-Margison, *Paulo Freire*, 47.
28. Mayo, *Gramsci, Freire and Adult Education*, 61–62.
29. Freire, *Pedagogy of the Oppressed*, 163.
30. Freire, *Pedagogy of Hope*, 38–39.
31. See Freire, "Conscientisation," 23.
32. Schipani, *Conscientization and Creativity*, ix.

Paulo Freire's Concept of Conscientização: A Commitment to Process

says that the word *conscientização* was born during a series of roundtable meetings of professors at the Brazilian Institute of Higher Studies, which was created after the "liberating" revolution of 1964 under the wing of the Ministry of Education. However, it was Dom Helder Cámara who popularized the term and gave it meaning in English.[33]

Freire expressed that *conscientização* is frequently taken to be synonymous with the French expression *prise de conscience* (become aware, first level of apprehension of reality).[34] For him, "conscientisation is possible only because *prise de conscience* is possible. If [human beings] were not able to become aware, there wouldn't be any conscientisation."[35] However, this *prise de conscience* is not yet *conscientização*. *Conscientização* is the critical development of a *prise de conscience*. "Thus, conscientisation is a probing of the ambience of reality. The more a person conscientises [oneself], the more [one] unveils reality and gets at the phenomenic essence of the object [one] stands in front of, to analyze it."[36] For that same reason, *conscientização* is a praxis. It joins action and reflection as two-paired, dialecticized elements permanently constituting that special way of being in the world (or transforming it) is peculiar to the human being.[37] In other words, *conscientização* is the process through which human beings achieve a deepened awareness both of the sociocultural reality and their capacity to transform that reality. Therefore, the process of *conscientização* is both individual and collective, and it involves action and reflection. It is important to mention that Freire understands *conscientização* as a process, not some method or technique. His concept of *conscientização* is founded upon a dialectical and phenomenological approach to the relationship between consciousness and the world. It requires intentionality, affirmation of the subjective-objective dialectic, consciousness, and conscious action on the objectivized reality.

Accordingly, for a better understanding of Freire's thinking, it is important to situate his pedagogy in the specific historical and political

---

33. Dom Helder Cámara (1909–1999) was the Archbishop of Recife during Freire's time. He gained an international reputation as a champion of human rights during the era of military dictatorship and as a dedicated champion for the poor. He toured the world denouncing the oppression in the Third World and drawing links between the gospel and liberation.

34. See Schipani, *Conscientization and Creativity*, chs. 1–2.

35. Freire, "Conscientisation," 24.

36. Freire, "Conscientisation," 25.

37. Freire, "Conscientisation," 25.

circumstances of neoliberalism and imperialism. Therefore, Freire's thought needs to be understood in the context of the political and economic situation of the Third World. His personal knowledge of extreme poverty and suffering challenged his ethical teaching and work, leading him to side with the oppressed.[38] It was in this context that Freire's epistemology framed the concept of *conscientização*, oppression, and dialogue, which are at the heart of his pedagogical endeavor.

THE WHY AND HOW OF *CONSCIENTIZAÇÃO*

Why is *conscientização* a core element in Freire's pedagogy? Freire's use of the term *conscientização* and his emphasis on human states of consciousness often exposed him as an idealist or dreamer because it seemed too simplistic to believe that with a change of consciousness, social change can occur. But it is clear that Freire's work was not just a product of theorization and years of studies but also of the many life experiences on the personal, occupational, and academic level, "limit-situations," as well as the impact of his own sociopolitical context.[39] All these were interweaving the heart of his pedagogy.

In his book *Pedagogy of Hope: Reliving Pedagogy of the Oppressed*, which was written in 1992, Freire reflects upon his experience from his earlier years and on what he wanted to articulate in *Pedagogy of the Oppressed*, which was meant as a criticism of sectarianism in defense of a critical radicalism.[40] Using a historical approach, what follows will present some of Freire's keystone experiences written in *Pedagogy of Hope* that led him to articulate his critical radicalism. My intention is to show how his own life experiences are intrinsically related to his development of *conscientização*.

---

38. One of many critiques of Freire is that he ideologized the oppressed. From a critical pedagogy point of view, Freire calls forth broad and mystical/idealistic abstractions which may be inspirational but do not engage with the issue of specific complexities of overlapping oppressions. "Who can argue with the dream of liberation that never reaches a plenitude?" See Weiler, "Myths of Paulo Freire," 370.

39. For Freire, "limit-situations" do not represent hopeless obstacles. Rather, they are problematic and conflicting circumstances which call for a resolution. "Limit-situations imply the existence of persons who are directly or indirectly served by situations, and of those who are negated and curved by them. Once the latter come to perceive these situations as the frontier between being and nothingness, they begin to direct their increasingly critical actions towards achieving the untested feasibility implicit in the perception." Freire, *Pedagogy of the Oppressed*, 102.

40. Freire, *Pedagogy of Hope*, 40.

Paulo Freire's Concept of Conscientização: A Commitment to Process

In 1947, at twenty-six years old, Freire was teaching Portuguese at Colégio Oswaldo Cruz, the same school where he completed his secondary education. He also was in the middle of his last year of law school and was working some cases as a creditor attorney. One day he was invited to work for the Serviço Social da Indústria. He was surprised by the appealing invitation but was not able to make a quick decision about taking that job. One afternoon he was talking to one of his clients, a young man, who had set up his own dental office and had not paid his debts, told Freire, "I made a mistake. I guess I was very optimistic. I took out a loan I can't pay back . . . so, well, sir . . . you can take our furniture . . . only you can't have my eighteen-month old baby girl."[41] This conversation changed the direction of Freire's life. He abandoned law that afternoon, said yes to SESI's summons to its Division of Education and Culture, and started his career as an educator.

Freire called his years in SESI a foundational time. He worked especially on relations between schools and families. At that time, he carried out a research project covering one-thousand families of students in Recife, Zona da Mata, and Pernambuco. The research consisted in asking questions about their relationship with their children, about forms of punishments, reasons for it, and rewards. After sifting through the results, Freire was astonished at the emphasis on violent corporal punishment.[42] This experience led him to start articulating and reflecting upon the political consequences of that kind of relationship between parents and children and between teachers and students, realizing that families and schools were subjected to a greater context of global society that was reproducing the authoritarian ideology. With this material, Freire wrote his dissertation, discussing the themes of authority, freedom, punishment, and reward.

Freire was determined to help those families. He did presentations using Jean Piaget's material to talk to the parents about a dialogical, loving relationship between parents and children instead of violent punishments, which led him to a keystone experience. In one of these presentations, a gentleman raised his hand to talk: "Some nice words from Dr. Paulo Freire . . . now I'd like to ask the doctor a couple of things . . . sir, do you know where people live?" The gentleman started describing the deplorable

---

41. Freire, *Pedagogy of Hope*, 9.

42. Some of the punishments described by Freire are tying a child to a tree, locking them in a room for hours, forcing them to kneel on stones used to grind corn, and thrashing them with leather straps. See Freire, *Pedagogia da Esperança*, 21.

conditions in which they were living and compared the space of Freire's house. He continued and compared differences when arriving home after a long day of work and said, "It's one thing to come home and find the kids all bathed . . . well fed, not hungry—and another thing to come home and find your kids dirty, hungry, crying . . . and people have to get up at four in the morning to start all over again. . . . If people hit their kids . . . it's not because people don't love their kids. No, it is because life is so hard that they don't have much choice."[43] Freire wanted to scrunch further down into his chair and disappear when listening to the words of this gentleman. That evening had a profound impact on Freire. This existential experience influenced the development of his pedagogical thought and educational practice. He wanted to develop a method based on dialogue with a horizontal relationship between persons, and he realized the importance of connecting knowledge with reality. Moreover, Freire's work with SESI developed a deeper sense of his vocation as educator. He realized that method was not the only necessary element to help those families. "Rather than worrying about method, [Freire] was always committed to teaching as an ontological vocation rather than as a technical academic responsibility."[44] Understanding teaching as an ontological vocation led him to incorporate two pedagogical principles: dialogue and collective work.[45]

Freire suffered depression during the ages of twenty-two and twenty-nine. Another keystone experience was confronting his depression. He began to see the framework in which the depression occurred, what preceded it the day before, what he heard or said. He took his depression as an object of curiosity and investigation. He realized it occurred during the rainy season when making trips to green farming zones and seeing *massapê* clay (black clay of the Northeast). One day he went to Jaboatão on a rainy afternoon to revisit his childhood. He stopped in front of the house in which he lived and where his father died. He remembered the scene of his dad dying. That rainy afternoon, with the dark sky over the green land and the ground soaked, Freire discovered the fabric of his depression. He unveiled the problem, the why of his pain, and the relationship between the rain, the green, and the sticky clay that sparked the depression. Unmasking the "why" of his suffering helped him to overcome it and was freed from a

---

43. Freire, *Pedagogy of Hope*, 17–18.
44. Dale and Hyslop-Margison, *Paulo Freire*, 49.
45. Souza, *Paulo Freire*, 21.

Paulo Freire's Concept of Conscientização: A Commitment to Process

limitation.⁴⁶ He also engaged reality with new lenses, rereading and redoing the world in a different way. This experience gave Freire a new insight: to devote himself to the SESI groups of workers, challenging them to read their own world and to speak their own reading. Many could have the possibility of unveiling the why for what they suffered (referring to a more critical knowledge of the domain of socioeconomic structures), but Freire reached a limit: "A more critical understanding of the situation of oppression does not yet liberate the oppressed."⁴⁷ It is a step in the right direction, but the person needs a new understanding that leads him or her to engage in a political struggle for the transformation of concrete conditions that make the oppression prevail. The practice of education does not itself effect the transformation of the world but implies it.

Due to the subversive educational work Freire conducted with workers during his time with SESI, helping them to awaken their consciousness to oppressive structures, he was arrested and subjected to long interrogations by military-police. He was exiled in September 1964.⁴⁸

The last key experience to be pointed out is his experience of exile where he culminated the main insights of his pedagogical work. Freire was in exile for almost sixteen years. In June 1980, he returned to reintegrate and live in his own country. He expressed that exile is a difficult experience, and it is far more difficult when not making the effort to adopt its space. "When you are in exile you live a borrowed life."⁴⁹

---

46. Freire's depression affected and threatened his professional activity, relationships, and life in community to the point that he was not engaged in the political struggle. Freire, *Pedagogia da Esperança*, 29.

47. Freire, *Pedagogy of Hope*, 23.

48. Though Freire was in exile, it is important to note that the effects of the military dictatorship weighed on him. Freire continued to be attuned to what was happening in Brazil. Correspondence with students, teachers, family, and friends was more intense during exile. Freire wanted to be connected to his own country and know about the educational work he had developed but could not continue in Brazil. Many of those with whom he worked from 1962 to 1964 (April 1, 1964, was the coup d'état, or *golpe de estado*, and was the time when the military coup put an end to Freire's educational effort) remained in Brazil. Some were persecuted, imprisoned, tortured, and killed due to their "subversive" ideas and work. Freire's work continued to be at the heart of the many forces of opposition that were endeavoring to raise the consciousness of the people, such as the Catholic Church and its base communities, bishops (like Dom Helder Camara), religious educators, journalists, and popular movements. Despite Freire's absence, his work and ideas remained. For further discussion on this topic, see Freire, *Cartas a Cristina*; and Freire, *Teachers as Cultural Workers*.

49. Freire, "Learning to Question," 196.

Toward a New, Praxis-Oriented Missiology

Freire arrived in La Paz, Bolivia, and shortly thereafter, the military coup drove him out to Chile. In Santiago, together with his family, he started a new phase of his life and work. He lived in that country from November 1964 to April 1969 and followed closely the ideological struggle of that time. He witnessed different reactions to political ideology: (1) persons who have proclaimed an option for the transformation of society became frightened and repentant, then became reactionaries; (2) persons who confirmed their progressive discourse by walking consistently, refusing to run from history; and (3) persons whose initial position was timid but who became more radical without succumbing to sectarianism. During those years in Chile, Freire worked in the Instituto de Desarollo Agropecuario, Chile's Ministry of Education, and also as a consultant to UNESCO with Chile's Instituto de Capacitacion en Reforma Agraria. He listened to peasants, discussed with them different aspects of their concrete reality, and urged agronomists and agricultural technologists to adapt the political, pedagogical, and democratic understanding of their practice. He supported the agrarian reform. While working with peasants, he discussed their rights to land, to freedom, to produce and to raise crops and livestock, to live decently and simply to be, to be respected as persons and as workers, and to have access to culture and knowledge. This experience not only gave him new insights about his educational work but also helped him to reflect and understand the political struggle of his own country. *Pedagogy of the Oppressed* took root in those historic-social conditions. During his years in Chile, he attempted to articulate the relationship between political lucidity in "a reading of the world" (that is, having a critical perception of one's own reality and environment), the different levels of engagement in the process of mobilization, and the organization for the struggle of the defense of rights and for laying claim to justice. Freire realized that struggle is a historical and social category; therefore, it has historicity.[50]

I did not mention Freire's experience living in Massachusetts and teaching at Harvard or his support of the Cuban revolution. Nor did I expound on the time he lived in Geneva and traveled around the world as a consultant in the department of education of the World Council of Churches, helping countries that had won their political independence to systematize their plans in education. Certainly, there are many more experiences that shaped Freire's thought and work that made him develop and realize the importance of *conscientização*. It is important to mention again

50. Freire, *Pedagogy of Hope*, 32.

Paulo Freire's Concept of Conscientização: A Commitment to Process

that Freire was also deeply influenced and enlightened by the philosophical currents of his time. However, the principal motor that kept Freire thinking and searching were the experiences of his life situations.

One could clearly see that it is important to grasp Freire's spirit and life experience when understanding *conscientização*. But is it worthwhile to continue looking at the heart of Freire's pedagogy in the twenty-first century? Is *conscientização* necessary nowadays? Though many critiques and questions remain regarding Freire's method, what follows will attempt to rescue its relevance. Having presented what deeply moved and shaped Freire's thought, I will lay out the most common way of learning Freire's pedagogy. The following will outline the three phases common to pre-literacy and post-literacy of Freire's educational proposal that led to the process of *conscientização*.[51] For this, I will use a diagram elaborated by Denis Collins.[52] The intention for presenting the structured steps of the process of *conscientização* is to raise the following question: By presenting a diagram that intends to summarize and capture an important content, could one grasp the depth of the intentionality of the process of *conscientização*?

1. Investigation

The first phase in the preparation of Freire's literacy program is the discovery of the "vocabulary universe" of the community, which is the vocabulary most commonly and typically expressed by the people, along with the full existential meaning that this vocabulary signifies for that community. For example, when Freire asked for the meaning and connection that people in a Third World country have with respect to specific words within their vocabulary universe, such as donkey, work, or factory, the response he would receive differed from those whom he might have asked from a First World country.[53] The investigation and examination of "generative words"—words derived from a people's vocabulary universe—present the associations people make with the words and the ways in which people perceive and access their reality. Freire describes this first level of consciousness as *naïve/magic consciousness*. Naïve or magic consciousness "simply

---

51. For the three phases to pre-literacy and post-literacy, see Freire, *Education for Critical Consciousness*, 37–49.

52. Collins, "Two Utopians," 128–30. Collins also handed me his personal notes that expand on the three phases common to pre-literacy and post-literacy of Freire's educational proposal.

53. See Schipani, *Conscientization and Creativity*, 5.

apprehends facts and attributes to them a superior power by which it is controlled and to which it must therefore submit. Magic consciousness is characterized by fatalism, which leads human beings to fold their arms, resigned to the impossibility of resisting the power facts."[54] The investigation phase's objective is to help the person with the examination and discovery of their less critical consciousness or consciousness as naïve.

2. *Thematization*

The thematic investigation consists not only of a study of the local reality or context but of the people's perception of their reality. The people's language and thought dialectically refer to their social reality.[55] The themes (for example, the theme of domination and liberation) of the epoch are constituted by representations of influential and common ideas, challenges, values, and hopes of the people as well as the obstacles to their full humanization.[56] For Freire, the "thematic universe" is the name for the complex themes that differ from one particular context to the other and always needs to be investigated once again; for instance, the theme of domination for a person living in *la favela* is different from a *campesino*, and what domination meant in the year 1970 for a *campesino* in Brazil is different from a *campesino* in California. Thus, the thematic universe in a given sociocultural setting is both a requirement and a feature of this process.[57] Freire's intention during this second phase is to choose situations that are familiar to the participants in order to facilitate their direct involvement, both as reflecting subjects and as objects of their own reflection. By reflecting on the "codification" of their own situations, people reveal their level of awareness regarding that reality. Then, with the help of the coordinators, they start a "decodification" process, which makes it possible to point out major conflicts and contradictions. The intention is to help the participations deal not just with partial representations of some sectors of their reality but with their total existential situation. For example, *el campesino puede describir su realidad cotidiana y hablar de los instrumentos que usa para desempeñar su trabajo en el campo, pero se le puede ayudar a pensar y cuestionarse porque a un campesino normalmente no se le ve con un libro en la mano.*[58] Thus, in

54. Freire, *Education for Critical Consciousness*, 39.
55. See Schipani, *Conscientization and Creativity*, 5.
56. See Freire, *Pedagogy of the Oppressed*, 101.
57. See Schipani, *Conscientization and Creativity*, 4.
58. Schipani, *Conscientization and Creativity*, 5. My translation is as follows: "The

Paulo Freire's Concept of Conscientização: A Commitment to Process

the thematization phase, the person is led to a deeper perception of their reality and therefore to a deeper level of *conscientização*.

3. Problematization

Freire's educational project attempted to move the people from naïve consciousness to a critical attitude. When people become aware of their "limit-situations" (rather than perceiving those situations as impossible obstacles), they are called to strive for a resolution. These become challenges for further growth and for being more human.[59] For Freire, it is then that a process of liberation truly begins.

Figure 2.1 presents Collins's diagram of the three phases common to pre-literacy and post-literacy from Freire's educational proposal.

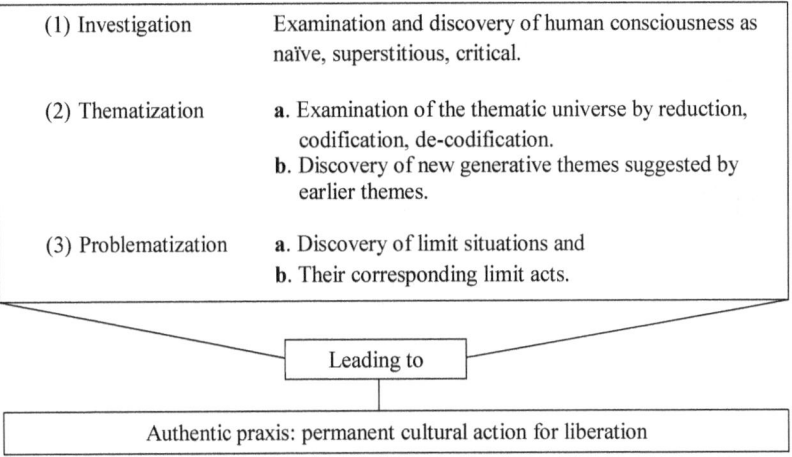

Figure 2.1. Freire's phases to pre-literacy and post-literacy.

Explaining the three phases of the process of *conscientização* is the most used method to teach people the revolutionary pedagogy of Freire, even by critical theory professors. In this way, there is the risk that the concept of *conscientização* gets reduced to a method or technique or simply as a very interesting concept to look at. Also, presenting it as a method or technique misses the collective or communitarian process it entails. At

---

farmer can describe his/her everyday reality and speak about the instruments he/she uses to work the field, but the person can be helped to think and to question why a farmer is not usually seen with a book in hand."

59. See Freire, *Pedagogy of the Oppressed*, 102.

Toward a New, Praxis-Oriented Missiology

the same time, the spirit or impetus that moved Freire to struggle for real individual democracy can become entrapped.

In order to find *conscientização* necessary and applicable to our present context, it is important to situate *conscientização* within life's experience and struggles: one's personal, work, academic, and specific sociopolitical context. Freire's own process of *conscientização* was sparked within the context of his life experience. Without this, *conscientização* is reduced to a method, technique, or a nice critical understanding. Moreover, Freire was always against importing or exporting his pedagogical practices. "I don't want to be imported or exported. It is impossible to export pedagogical practices without reinventing them. Please tell my fellow American educators not to import me. Ask them to re-create, reinvent, and rewrite my ideas."[60]

FREIRE'S UNDERSTANDING OF REALITY[61]

Since the process of *conscientização* begins with a perception of reality and seeks the transformation of it, it is important to understand how Freire defines reality. One can perceive how Freire's work and thought is permeated by his philosophical background in the area of phenomenology and psychology of language.

For Freire, the world of human beings, animals, living things, and inanimate things do not exist without the "knower human being" who is capable of the perception of reality. Human beings never exist apart from the world, and their relationship with the world is unique. It is revolutionary to become aware that it is possible to orient and impact the world by an act of knowing and through thought-language. It is important to remark that within Freire's thought, the centrality of the process of orientation to reality is through critical reflection and thought-language. This is because the process of knowing and naming subjectivity and objectivity are united.[62] The following will identify and explain key ideas in Freire's understanding of reality.

---

60. Araújo Freire and Macedo, *Paulo Freire Reader*, 6.

61. For this section, I will use Collins, *Paulo Freire: Filosofía Educativa*, ch. 2; and Collins, *Paulo Freire: His Life*. Both texts describe Freire's dialectical thought as well as his theory of reality and theory of knowledge/epistemology.

62. Collins, *Paulo Freire: Filosofía Educativa*, 204.

a) Reality is experienced as a process

Reality can easily be fragmented by believing that only the self is all that can be known to exist (solipsism) or determined by human beings, nature, and things by physical or biological processes alone (mechanistic objectivism). In this way, we reduce human beings and the world to things or to abstractions and miss discovering reality as process. Freire believed that human beings possess the ability to participate and intervene in the historical process and that transformation is the ability of human beings "to be more." Human beings can "be more" as they view reality as a totality and act in it through critical reflection to transform it.[63]

b) Thought-language enables human beings to understand themselves in relation to their world[64]

"Reality is non-dualistic and implies constant interaction between [a human being] as a thinking subject and history and culture."[65] It is important to mention that Freire does not separate objectivity from subjectivity. Human beings are both cause and effect of history and culture, and when they deny the opportunity to engage in an authentic thought-language to transform history, they become alienated from reality. Freire uses thought-language as a unity that mediates the world to the human being since thought is impossible without a language, and both are impossible without the world to which they refer. For Freire, the human word is a combination of thought and action to humanize history and culture.[66]

c) Human beings are the only beings who have relationships with the world

Human beings are in and with the world and have the capacity to reflect.[67] The consciousness and actions of human beings are historical and give dimension to their relationships with the world into periods that indicate the here, now, past, and future. Human beings created history and are created by history. Only human beings can act with intention and are able to reflect

---

63. Collins, *Paulo Freire: Filosofía Educativa*, 205.
64. Collins, *Paulo Freire: Filosofía Educativa*, 205–6.
65. Collins, *Paulo Freire: Filosofía Educativa*, 206.
66. See Freire, *Pedagogy of the Oppressed*, 87–89.
67. Collins, *Paulo Freire: Filosofía Educativa*, 206.

and discover the contradictions of reality and discover reality as a problem to be transformed. Therefore, only human beings are capable of praxis and are able to create. According to Freire, human beings who are not critical never achieve an integration with the world. Human beings are reflective, determined and determining, challenged, self-reflective, and capable to commit to the project to become historical.[68]

d) Distinguishing between "live" and "exist"[69]

For Freire, existence is a state of being that some human beings do not enjoy. Animals merely live and human beings are meant to exist.[70] Freire's reflection points out the difference between living and existing. The oppressed, by denying their right to name the world and to direct their relationship with the world, are denied the right to "have," which is a condition for all human beings to "exist." The oppressed are reduced to a state of being for another and become an object for the oppressor. Therefore, the oppressor does not take into consideration that the necessity to "have" is a condition for all human beings to "exist" but insists upon his or her own privilege to have more and thus cease to exist. Freire sees that the oppressor also starts living in a dehumanized state—dehumanizing themselves and the people they oppress. For him, both humanization and dehumanization are possibilities for a person, but while both are real alternatives, only humanization is the people's vocation.[71]

---

68. Freire, "Pedagogy of Hope," 237–64.

69. Collins, *Paulo Freire: Filosofía Educativa*, 207.

70. It is important to mention that the twenty-first century has developed more awareness about the care of the earth and the care of animals. The intention here is not to diminish animal theology or recent studies on animals where researchers have realized that animals have thought processes, emotions, and social connections that are as important to them as they are to us. Freire uses the context of his time when expressing the difference between living and existing. For more information about how animals think and feel, see Worrall, "Yes, Animals Think and Feel."

71. For Freire, there is an anthropological concern in which the people as beings in the world have a constant preoccupation with "what" and "how" they are "being." Freire states that the established institutions attempt to affirm human beings as the subject of decisions. Therefore, this could be the beginning of dehumanization, which brings the consequences of injustice, exploitation, oppression, and violence. See Freire, *Pedagogy of the Oppressed*, ch. 1.

e) Human existence is a task of praxis[72]

The ability of human beings to reflect upon reality as subjects, to be the author of their own reflections and to authenticate their relationships with the world, unveils the relationship between human being-world and the subjects themselves as unfinished tasks. Freire borrows the term praxis from Marx: action has to be combined with reflection. Through reflective activities with actions, human beings give meaning to history and culture. If the person is content with mere reflections (theorizing about relationships with the world), that person limits oneself to verbalism (sacrifice of action). Alternatively, if the person fails to reflect when acting, that person limits oneself to activism (sacrifice of reflection).[73] Neither verbalism nor activism is real praxis. Praxis always combines reflection with action to create the human world of ideas, symbols, language, science, religion, art, and production.

f) Within history, human beings are "unfinished"[74]

The world is not finished. It is always in the process of becoming. The human being, too, is in process. Freire holds that as a historical and cultural being experiences oneself as conditioned, it implies a being who becomes: "In my unfinishedness I know that I am conditioned. Yet conscious of such conditioning, I know that I can go beyond it, which is the essential difference between conditioned and determined existence."[75] Freire states that in this condition of being, dialectical opposites are expressed: *ser* (to be) and *estar siendo* (to be-becoming).

g) The human being has a vocation: to become a subject

Freire believed that the ontological vocation of human beings is to become fully human.[76] If human beings reflect on themselves, they could

---

72. Collins, *Paulo Freire: Filosofía Educativa*, 207.
73. See Freire, *Pedagogy of the Oppressed*, 89.
74. Collins, *Paulo Freire: Filosofía Educativa*, 208.
75. Freire, *Pedagogy of Freedom*, 54.
76. For Freire, simply to be human is to have an ontological vocation. In the section on Freire's philosophical influence, we saw Sartre's and Heidegger's influence on Freire. As a matter of fact, Freire was a student of Sartre. Therefore, Freire's understanding of vocation is another word for "work," which has a connotative meaning of work in a spiritual context or as accompanied by a calling in accordance with an individual's higher nature. Work is a word for doing, and ontology is a word for being, becoming what you are not

make three discoveries: (1) they are capable of reflecting upon their reflections, (2) they are "in" a situation, and (3) they are becoming. These discoveries and the constant process of reflection on oneself and one's situatedness are operations proper to subjects. Human beings must re-create themselves as subjects by continual reflection.[77] As subjects, human beings are empowered to interact with the world. As mentioned in section (b), Freire does not separate objectivity from subjectivity. When both are united through authentic actions in transforming the world, human beings become the creator and author of history. "My role in the world is not simply that of someone who registers what occurs but of someone who has an input into what happens."[78]

h) To exist is to act politically for hominization[79]

For Freire, the world is revealed in a dialectical social structure composed of an infrastructure that is the result of the human being's work and his or her relationship to the world, giving it meaning and a political superstructure which expresses the infrastructure. The only way to exist (to be fully human) is to act upon the world so that the dialectic of permanence and change is preserved in the social structure. This implies the critical reflective process by which human beings overcome limit-situations.[80] Freire's pedagogical work emphasizes no-neutrality and insists that true education must lead to a revolutionary activity. For Freire, to exist is to take political action in favor of hominization.

---

yet. For Freire, as for Sartre, there is no being apart from doing, as being only exists in relation to the other in action moving forward in time. Ontological vocation is the best word to bring about the best state of being that accepts our "throw-ness" in the world (what Sartre calls our "facticity") while at the same time striving to embody the openness to the new that is our true shared nature. Education in this context elevates us beyond our biology and toward our humanity. See Morrow and Torres, *Reading Freire and Habermas*, 62.

77. See Collins, *Paulo Freire: Filosofía Educativa*, 209.

78. Freire, *Pedagogy of Freedom*, 74.

79. Hominization refers to the process of a person reaching his or her full potential as a human being. The term is used in different contexts in the fields of paleontology and paleoanthropology, archeology, philosophy, and theology. Collins, *Paulo Freire: Filosofía Educativa*, 211.

80. The lack of literacy skills together with other limiting existential conditions is perceived by Freire as limit-situations. Recall that limit-situations do not represent hopeless obstacles. They are rather problematic circumstances which call for a resolution. Freire, *Pedagogy of the Oppressed*, 102.

Paulo Freire's Concept of Conscientização: A Commitment to Process

In summary, Freire's notion of reality is intrinsically connected to action. This perception implies a relationship with the world and the action one can take to transform it. Therefore, for Freire, the process of *conscientização* cannot take place without such a perception of reality.

WHAT ARE THE AIMS OF FREIRE'S *CONSCIENTIZAÇÃO*?

Why did Freire's method meet with such success? Why was it able to eventually reach 2,000,000 people who could not read or write? What made it appealing for *campesinos* who worked from dawn to dusk but attended the session every night for forty-five days? Freire had a specific aim when teaching thousands of peasants how to read and write: to lead them through a process of *conscientização*. The following will present the intended aims of the process of *conscientização*.

a) Education for Freedom

Freire was fully convinced that education, as an exercise in freedom, is an act of knowing and a critical approach to reality.[81] According to Freire, education is the most important value-means for the process of human liberation.[82] Freire's ontology and epistemology stress that the relationship between human being-world is mediated by thought-language. Since thought-language is alienated by the historical situation of oppression, the relationship between human being-world is alienated and oppressed.[83] For Freire, to move away from this oppressed consciousness and alienated living requires political power (power is in the possession of the oppressors).

---

81. See Collins, *Paulo Freire: Filosofía Educativa*, 232.

82. One of the major criticisms of using Freire's pedagogical method has to do with the assumption that Freire's liberating educational processes will be transformative when there is rich proof to the contrary. This is not a criticism of the liberating educational processes but a failure to take into account the prevalent and seductive forces (economic, cultural, political, religious, etc.) to which individuals and groups give themselves over, not by force but by choice, despite the liberating educating processes to which they have been exposed.

83. Freire was also influence by Lev Vygotsky's work. Vygotsky developed a sociocultural approach to cognitive development. His theories stress the fundamental role of social interaction in the development of cognition, as he believed strongly that community plays a central role in the process of "making meaning." Vygotsky argued that "learning is a necessary and universal aspect of the process of developing culturally organized, specifically human psychological function." In other words, social learning tends to precede development. Vygotsky, *Mind in Society*, 90. See also Rogoff, *Apprenticeship in Thinking*, 25–41.

Toward a New, Praxis-Oriented Missiology

The oppressed lack political power, and therefore their educational activity cannot be simply technical. It follows that education for freedom on the part of the oppressed aims toward authentic consciousness-raising and cultural action to transform the social structures.[84]

b) *Cultural Action for Liberation*

Freire sees culture as the result of human beings' labor and their efforts to create and re-create. Culture is a systematic acquisition of human experience but as creative assimilation, not as information storing. It is important that the person discovers herself or himself to be a maker of the world of culture. All of us, whether literate or illiterate, have creative and re-creative impulses. Freire gives the example of the work of a sculptor, painter, mystic, or philosopher to show that culture is a human creation. "Acquiring literacy does not involve memorizing sentences, words, or syllables—lifeless objects unconnected to an existential universe—but rather an attitude of creation and re-creation, a self-transformation producing a stance of intervention in one's context."[85] According to Freire's thought, nobody educates anybody else and nobody educates oneself. Instead, people educate one another through their interactions with the world. In reality, the invention of our existence is developed through our interaction with the material world at our disposal. Freire advocated for a theory and practice based on an authentic dialogue. Such dialogue centers on the learners' existential situations and leads not only to the acquisition of literacy skills but also to the awareness of their right as human beings to transform reality.[86]

> What is cultural action? What is a cultural revolution? In generic terms, but in the good sense of the phrase, it is the way we culturally attack culture. It means that we see culture always as a problem and do not let it become static, becoming a myth and mystifying us. . . . At that moment our act of knowing illuminates the action that is the source of our knowing. And right there we have the permanent, constant, dynamic of our attitude toward culture itself.[87]

---

84. Collins, *Paulo Freire: Filosofía Educativa*, 233.
85. Freire, *Education for Critical Consciousness*, 45.
86. Freire, *Cultural Action for Freedom*, 13.
87. One can see that Freire's concept of culture is dynamic, and it requires human beings' action (efforts to create and re-create). For Freire, through reflective activities with actions, human beings give meaning to history and culture. Freire, "Concientisation," 26.

c) Denouncing and Announcing

One of the intended objectives of *conscientização* is to denounce the dehumanizing structures and to announce a structure that will humanize. Freire considered that utopian people can be prophetic and hopeful. Only those who announce and denounce, who are permanently committed to a radical process of transforming the world so that human beings can be more, can be prophetic.

> Reactionary people, oppressors cannot be Utopian, they cannot be prophetic, and because they cannot be prophetic they cannot have hope. What future has the oppressor but to preserve his present status as oppressor? What scope for denouncing can oppressors have, other than the denunciation of those who denounce them? What do oppressors have to announce but the announcement of their myths? And what can be the hope of those who have no future?[88]

For Freire, the utopian posture denounces oppressors and announces that the historical vocation of human beings is to be fully human. Moreover, thinking of tomorrow is engaging in prophecy.

> Prophets are those who are founded in what they live, in what they see, hear, apprehend, in what they understand, who are rooted in their epistemological curiosity exercise, alert to the signs they seek to comprehend, supported in their reading of the world and of words new and old, which is the base of how much they expose themselves, thus becoming more and more a presence in the world at a par with their time.[89]

Freire insisted that announcing, the prophetic activity of prophets, is not possible without denouncing and that neither would be possible without taking position before what human beings "are being" or "have been." For Freire, human nature constitutes itself socially and historically. Human beings by nature are inclined to intervene in the world and, as a result, make history. For Freire, this intervention in the world demands announcing and denouncing unjust structures.[90] Moreover,

> o pensamento profético, que é também utópico, implica a denúncia de como estamos vivendo e o anúncio de como poderíamos viver. É

---

88. Freire, "Conscientisation," 28.
89. Freire, *Pedagogy of Indignation*, 104.
90. Freire, *Pedagogia da Indignação*, 119–20.

Toward a New, Praxis-Oriented Missiology

> *um pensamento esperançoso, por isso mesmo. É neste sentido que, como o entendo, o pensamento profético não apenas fala do que pode vir, mas falando de como está sendo a realidade, denunciando-a, anuncia um mundo melhor.*[91]

For Freire, the more we are conscientized, the more we become fully human and commit to be announcers and denouncers for a better world. This commitment ought to be permanent, because denouncing and announcing has no yesterday, today, or tomorrow. Prophetic activity cannot be static because it is an ongoing effort for change.

d) Conscientização *and* Utopia

For Freire, utopia does not mean something unrealizable nor is it a form of idealism. "Utopia is the dialectization in the acts of denouncing and announcing—denouncing the dehumanizing structure and announcing the structure that will humanize."[92] Freire sees that *conscientização* clearly has to do with utopia. The more we are conscientized, the more we become announcers and denouncers and commit to changing things. This commitment should be permanent, because if we were to stop being utopian, we would simply bureaucratize ourselves. This is the danger inherent in any revolution. According to Freire, one skillful way to avoid that danger is by a cultural revolution: dialectization, which is ongoing since our situation can always be improved and changed.[93]

Freire experienced how the neoliberal discourse and its educational practice in Brazil was a systematic refusal of dreams and of utopia, a refusal that sacrifices hope. "*A morte do sonho e da utopia, prolongamento consequente da morta História, implica a imobilização da História na redução do futuro à permanência do presente.*"[94] Without dreams and without utopia,

---

91. Freire, *Pedagogia da Indignação*, 118–19. An English translation of the quote, though lacking the nuances of the Portuguese, is rendered as follows: "Prophetic thought, which is also utopian, implies *denouncing* how we are living and *announcing* how we could live. It is, for this very reason, a hope-filled form of thought. In this sense, prophetic thought, as I see it, not only speaks of what may come, but while speaking about reality as it is and *denouncing it*, also *announces* a better world." Freire, *Pedagogy of Indignation*, 105.

92. Freire, "Conscientisation," 28.

93. Freire, "Conscientisation," 26.

94. Freire, *Pedagogia da Indignação*, 123. An English translation, again lacking the nuances expressed in Portuguese, can be rendered as follows: "The death of dreams and utopia, a consequent extension of the death of history, implies the immobilization of

all that is left is technicality. Therefore, Freire insisted that *conscientização* is an appropriating of reality; and for that reason, for the utopian tension that permeates it, one can call it a reshaping of reality.

> In its strict sense, utopia is a projection of some state of affair not yet realized but which guides thought and action. It represents a place of "nowhere" since it does not exist and therefore remains unrecognizable in the concrete sense. By definition, utopian thinking is a critique of "reality," even a distortion of it in the positive sense. As a form of distortion, utopia attempts to represent reality as better than itself, as having reconciled its tensions and contradictions.[95]

Conscientização then is the most critical approach to reality, stripping it down so as to get to know the myths that deceive and perpetuate the dominating structure.[96]

We can say that *conscientização* is attained when education aims toward authentic consciousness-raising and cultural action to transform the social structures; when the invention of our existence is developed through our interaction with the material world at our disposal, producing a stance for intervention in one's context; when those who are permanently committed to a radical process of transforming the world do not stop the prophetic call of announcing and denouncing so that human beings can be more; and when we do not stop being utopian because there is an ongoing effort for change.

e) Commitment in Time—Historical Commitment

For Freire, *conscientização* is also a commitment in time; in fact, there is no *conscientização* without historical commitment. So *conscientização* is also a historical awareness. It is a critical insertion into history. It means that human beings take on a role as subjects making the world and remaking the world. It asks human beings to fashion their existence out of the material that life offers them. The more they are conscientized, the more they exist.[97]

Conscientização implies that when a person realizes that she or he is oppressed, that person also knows that liberation is possible if one transforms

---

history within a reduction of the future to permanence of the present." Freire, *Pedagogy of Indignation*, 110.

95. Leonardo, "Reality on Trial," 504.
96. Freire, "Conscientisation," 27.
97. Freire, "*Conscientisation*," 25.

the concrete situation where one finds oneself oppressed. Obviously, we cannot transform that reality just in our head. For Freire, that would be to fall into the idealist philosophical error of thinking that awareness creates reality. The consequence would simply be announcing we are free just with our minds, and yet the structures would continue to be the same as ever so that we would not be free. Instead, *conscientização* implies a critical insertion into a process; it implies a historical commitment to make changes. That is why *conscientização* offers us to adopt a utopian attitude toward the world, an attitude that turns the conscientized into a utopian agent.

Freire clearly unveiled his passion for education and transforming the world. I would like to conclude this section with Freire's words that collect the aim of *conscientização*:

> Conscientisation could never be an imposition on others or a manipulation of them. I cannot impose my opinions on someone else. I can only invite them to share, to discuss. To impose on others my way of not being would be a real contradiction. For loving is not only a free act, it is an act for freedom. And love that cannot produce more freedom is not love.[98]

CONSCIENTIZAÇÃO AND DIALOGUE

Conscientização suggests the capacity not only for understanding one's reality; others' mutual understanding is key to transforming, reordering, and reconciling relationships. No matter how reflective or practice-based *conscientização* is, it is not sufficient or an end in itself. If *conscientização* is uncoupled from the process of dialogue, it cannot, in and of itself, lead to any kind of transformation. Therefore, for Freire, dialogue is an essential tool to help the person become a subject and not an object or political tool for real democratization.

Freire's process of *conscientização* is based on *dialogue*, which is a *horizontal* relationship between persons where there is a relationship of empathy between the two parties. Dialogue creates a critical attitude, and yet only dialogue truly communicates. This is in opposition with *anti-dialogue*, which according to Freire has been part of our historical-cultural formation. Anti-dialogue involves *vertical* relationships between persons; therefore, it is acritical and cannot create a critical attitude. In anti-dialogue, the relationship of empathy between the parties is broken.

---

98. Freire, *"Conscientisation,"* 31.

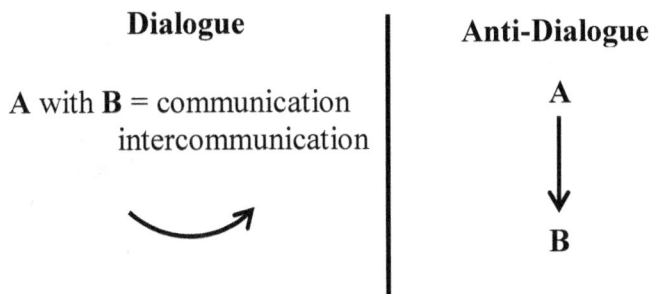

Figure 2.2 Freire's understanding of dialogue and anti-dialogue.

For Freire, anti-dialogue violates the nature of human beings and their process of discovery, and it contradicts democracy. However, dialogue presupposes maturity, a spirit of adventure, confidence in questioning, and seriousness in providing answers.[99] Additionally, authentic dialogue promotes participation and democracy.[100] "*E impossível só falar em participação sem experimentá-la. Não podemos aprender a nadar nesta sala. Temos de ir até a água. Democracia é a mesma coisa: aprende-se democracia fazendo democracia.*"[101]

Freire's analysis of dialogue is powerful. For him, the essence of dialogue is *the word*. The word is more than just an instrument that makes dialogue possible. Within the word, Freire describes two dimensions: reflection and action. "There is no true word that is not at the same time a praxis. Thus, to speak a true word is to transform the world."[102] For Freire, human existence cannot be silent nor can it be nourished by false words but only by true words with which human beings can transform the world. Dialogue is the encounter between human beings, mediated by the world, in order to name the world. Therefore, dialogue is an existential necessity.

> *Como posso dialogar, se alieno a ignorância, isto é, se a vejo sempre no outro, nunca em mim? Como posso dialogar, se me admito como um homem diferente, virtuoso por herança, diante dos outros, meros*

99. Freire, *Pedagogy of the Heart*, 99.

100. See Freire, *Cartas a Cristina*, 164–77.

101. Freire and Shor, *Medo e Ousadia*, 60. My translation is as follows: "It is impossible only speak of participation without experience it. We cannot learn to swim in this room. We need to go to the water. Democracy is the same thing: we learn democracy experiencing democracy."

102. Freire, *Pedagogy of the Oppressed*, 87.

Toward a New, Praxis-Oriented Missiology

> "isto", em que não reconheço outros eu? Como posso dialogar, se me sinto participante de um "gueto" de homens puros, donos da verdade e do saber, para quem todos os que estão fora são "essa gente", ou são "nativos inferiores"? Como posso dialogar, se parto de que a pronúncia do mundo é tarefa de homens seletos e que a presença das massas na história é sinal de sua deterioração que devo evitar? Como posso dialogar, se me fecho à contribuição dos outros, que jamais reconheço, e até me sinto ofendido com ela? Como posso dialogar se temo a superação e se, só em pensar nela, sofro e definho?[103]

Freire echoes Karl Jaspers's thought in asserting that dialogue constitutes the essence of societal structure and societal change:

> Dialogue is the only way, not only in the vital questions of political order, but in all the expressions of our being. Only by virtue of faith, however, does dialogue have power and meaning: by faith in [human beings] and [their] possibilities, by the faith that I can only become truly myself when other people also become themselves.[104]

Only dialogue externalizes and expresses itself socially, because in dialogue there is not just me, there is always another, there is always a "you." Freire proposes that dialogue should be "loving, humble, hopeful, trusting, and critical."[105] Dialogue cannot exist without humility; re-creating/transforming

---

103. Freire, *Pedagogia do Oprimido*, 47–48. The English translation of *Pedagogy of the Oppressed* misses the meaning of some of the words in Portuguese. For example, in the first question, the literal translation of *alieno a ignorância* is "to alienate ignorance." In the English translation of *Pedagogy of the Oppressed*, one will read, "I always project ignorance" in order to offer to the reader a better meaning of the phrase. However, Freire did not use the verb "to project" but "to alienate." Nevertheless, here is the rest of the English translation of the text: "How can I dialogue if I always project ignorance onto others and never perceive my own? How can I dialogue if I regard myself as a case apart from others—mere 'its' in whom I cannot recognize other 'I's? How can I dialogue if I consider myself a member of the in-group of 'pure' men, the owners of truth and knowledge, for whom all non-members are 'these people' or 'the great unwashed'? How can I dialogue if I start from the premise that naming the world is the task of an elite and that the presence of the people in history is a sign of deterioration, thus to be avoided? How can I dialogue if I am closed to—and even offended by—the contribution of others? How can I dialogue if I am afraid of being displaced, the mere possibility causing me torment and weakness?" Freire, *Pedagogy of the Oppressed*, 90.

104. Freire, *Education for Critical Consciousness*, 40. See also Jaspers, "Communication," 73–79.

105. Freire, *Education for Critical Consciousness*, 40–41.

the world cannot be an act of arrogance.[106] Furthermore, for Freire, dialogue requires faith in humankind, faith in the power to make and remake, to create and to re-create, and faith in the vocation of being fully human. In other words, this would assert that without dialogue one cannot be human.

Dialogue also involves respect and openness. It should not involve one person acting on another but rather people working with each other. It is the essence of education as freedom in practice.[107] Authentic dialogue recognizes that everyone has something to impart and something to learn. For Freire, mutual learning is essential in the process of *conscientização*. Finally, dialogue cannot exist without hope. Hopelessness itself is a form of silence. However, as long as we fight, we are moved by hope; and if we fight with hope, we can wait.[108]

CONCLUDING THOUGHTS

In order to find *conscientização* necessary and applicable to our present context, it is essential to situate *conscientização* within life's experience and struggles: one's personal, work, academic, and specific sociopolitical context. As previously discussed, Freire's own process of *conscientização* was sparked within the context of his life experience. Without taking this context into account, *conscientização* becomes merely a method or technique to admire. To mitigate against setting *conscientização* aside to the world of ideas, Freire did not want his pedagogical practices to be copied and

106. Freire believed that dialogue carries not only the capacity to be fully human but also the potential for creativity. In fact, he did some "spoken" books with the intention to commit himself to the task of creative work to overcome the temptation to be always alone and to write alone and instead to be in dialogue. For Freire, the exercise of spoken books was meaningful and a valuable intellectual exercise. His spoken books were done with the help of other scholars, for example, *Medo e Ousadia: O Cotidiano do Professor*, which has not been translated in other languages. It is a book in a form of dialogue with Ira Shor. Also, Freire spoke the book *Learning to Question: A Pedagogy of Liberation*, which is a powerful dialogue between him and Antonio Faundez. Both of them were living in Geneva at the time they spoke the book because both of them were exiled from their own countries due to the subversive educational work they were doing. See Freire and Faundez, *Learning to Question*.

107. Freire, *Pedagogy of Freedom*, 65.

108. We have seen that *conscientização* is a process that has the potential to transform reality through education. However, this possibility of transformation is not guaranteed, especially when other forces and power dynamics impede, compete with, or subvert the process. For example, corruption, gangs, narcotrafficking, globalization, terrorism, etc. make dialogue impossible. Therefore, a *conscientização* that does not give rise to dialogue is a nonproductive dead end, even an exercise in futility.

pasted. Instead, he asked others to understand and undergo the process of *conscientização* within their own particular reality and context.

It is also clear that the process of *conscientização* is both individual and collective and that it involves action and reflection. It is crucial to emphasize that Freire understands *conscientização* as a process that continuously unfolds.[109] As mentioned above, *conscientização* is based upon a dialectical and phenomenological approach to how consciousness and the world interact. It requires intentionality and consciousness. It affirms the subjective-objective dialectic. It also calls human beings to act consciously on the objectivized reality.

Furthermore, Freire's pedagogy should be understood within the specific historical and political circumstances from which it developed, namely, neoliberalism and imperialism. In other words, Freire's thought needs to be situated in the context of the political and economic situation of the Third World. His personal encounter with extreme poverty and suffering led him to reorient his pedagogical work in favor of the oppressed. The aims of *conscientização—education for freedom, cultural action for liberation, denouncing, announcing, utopia, and historical commitment*—show not only Freire's philosophical influence but also his restlessness to change the unjust socialpolitical structures and give voice to the voiceless. It was in the context of the Third World's political and economic situation that Freire's epistemology discussed the concept of *conscientização*, oppression, and dialogue, which are at the heart of his pedagogical endeavor.

Although *conscientização* is reflective and practice-based, it is not sufficient or an end in itself. If *conscientização* is uncoupled from the process of dialogue, it cannot in and of itself lead to any kind of transformation. Dialogue is necessary to spark and unfold a process of *conscientização*. Authentic dialogue acknowledges that we are constant learners, recognizing that everyone has something to impart and something to learn since we are unfinished human beings.

Lastly, the dialectic of becoming aware of our unfinishedness or incompleteness was also important to Freire. In Freire's last book before his death, *Pedagogy of Freedom*, he writes, "I like being human because in my unfinishedness I know that I am conditioned. Yet, conscious of such conditioning, I know that I can go beyond it, which is the essential

---

109. "Unfold" can be translated into Spanish as *desplegarse, revelar para*. The meaning of *desplegarse* describes an unfolding process that is not automatically given. Two images which come to mind are a rose in bloom and a mother bird teaching her young to fly.

Paulo Freire's Concept of Conscientização: A Commitment to Process

difference between conditioned and determined existence."[110] Freire's sense of unfinishedness does not have a negative connotation but a possibility of the "construction of my presence in the world, which is a construction involving others."[111] This incompleteness does not only give us the force to be in a constant movement of searching. The awareness of being unfinished is what makes us educable, and this same awareness makes us eternally seekers of hope. For Freire, hope is not just a question of courage but an ontological dimension of our human condition.[112]

Having looked at the heart of Freire's pedagogy, the following chapter will demonstrate how Freire's work on *conscientização* can be a tool for mission praxis. It will also compare Freire's and Bevans's work and how *conscientização* can be enriched by prophetic dialogue and vice versa.

---

110. *Pedagogy of Freedom: Ethics, Democracy, and Civic Courage*, with the original title in Portuguese *Pedagogia da Autonomia: Saberes Necessários 'a Prática Educativa*, was the last book written by Freire for the graduate seminar on liberation pedagogy that he and Donaldo Macedo were scheduled to teach at the Harvard Graduate School of Education (HGSE) during the 1997 fall semester. As they were preparing the seminar, Freire was concerned that institutions like HGSE were preponderantly hiding their ideology for scientific rigor and absolute objectivity, which leads to the fragmentation of knowledge because of the reductionist view of the act of knowing. Freire's intuition about Harvard's interest in his ideas and work was purely a matter of public relations. On May 2, 1997, Freire died of heart failure. Macedo expressed that Freire's death unveiled the hidden ideology that shaped HGSE and affirmed Freire's intuition. It was acceptable for one semester to legitimize openness, diversity, and democracy, but it was not acceptable to allow Freire's ideas to become part of their teaching. Macedo insisted to offer the seminar to honor Freire's legacy and to invite major Freirean scholars, like Bell Hooks or Peter McLaren, but the school canceled the seminar on liberation pedagogy. The seminar was intended for students that were preparing to be teachers. Freire's intention was to transmit what teachers need to know and be able to do in teaching and learning, focusing on education for equity, transformation, and inclusion of all individuals. Freire highlighted fundamental "knowledges" (*saberes*) that all teaches should have or at least be exposed to but were seldom thought in their preparation as teachers: "Teaching requires a recognition that education is ideological," "teaching always involves ethics," "teaching requires a capacity to be critical," "teaching requires the recognition of our conditioning," "teaching requires humility," and "teaching requires critical reflection," among others. See Macedo, foreword to *Pedagogy of Freedom*, xi–xxxii; Serpa and Serpa, review of *Pedagogia da Autonomia*; Freire, *Pedagogy of Freedom*, 54.

111. Freire, *Pedagogy of Freedom*, 56.

112. Freire, *Pedagogy of Freedom*, 58.

3

Conscientização Enhances Prophetic Dialogue and Vice Versa

> I like being human
> because I am involved with others
> in making history out of possibility.
>
> —Paulo Freire, *Pedagogy of Freedom*

This chapter will evaluate how far and by what means Freire's work on *conscientização* can enrich Bevans's work on prophetic dialogue and vice versa. It will not offer a new methodology or pedagogy to do mission. Rather, this chapter will put into dialogue these two thinkers to rescue the inherent transformative and liberating process that prophetic dialogue and *conscientização* entail. Furthermore, this chapter will emphasize process. In ministerial or missionary work, it is easy to pay attention to or focus on the end results, forgetting the seed of a gentle process that unfolds (or not) in the person and in society. Moreover, as we have seen in chapter 1, Bevans says that prophetic dialogue is a process. Similarly, in chapter 2 we saw how Freire emphasizes *conscientização* as a process.

In order to perceive the novelty of putting into dialogue Freire's concept of *conscientização* and Bevans's understanding of mission as prophetic dialogue, I will first offer a brief historical awareness of missionary methods so that the relevance of the pedagogical implications of Bevans's and Freire's contributions can be better grasped. Since the main component of Christian mission is the transmission of Christian faith, some relevant aspects in the

Conscientização Enhances Prophetic Dialogue and Vice Versa

transmission of Christian faith focusing on the experiential aspect of it will be presented. Lastly, this chapter will show how Bevans's and Freire's work enhance each other and will reveal some similarities in their work.

HISTORICAL AWARENESS OF MISSIONARY METHODS

Generally, talk about mission faces two fundamental questions: (1) the "why" of mission, which gives us the dogmatic, biblical, and ethical basis for the mission enterprise, and (2) the "how" of mission, which encompasses the way we approach and do mission.[1] The focus of this section is on the "how." This section will attempt to present the increased awareness of more adequate mission methods and some contemporary challenges that mission praxis faces.

As mentioned in chapter 1, mission is not an innocent word. Christians carry a painful history of Christianization for not using adequate methods for transmitting the Christian message in specific contexts, especially in places like Africa, Asia, and Latin America. Vincent Donovan gives the example of how the missionaries who came to East Africa over a century ago were facing the problem of slavery. The missionaries were concerned with doing something about the slavery system. They bought the slaves. So their pedagogical implication was buying slaves and Christianizing them.[2] Some of the most known critiques to missionary methods have been the following: (a) insensitivity toward individuals, societies, and cultures of specific contexts, which led to missionary approaches that were more imposing rather than inviting, (b) discrepancy between the content of faith and the way it is transmitted and lived, and (c) the "neglected" use of the Bible in mission.[3]

Protestant missiologists have done a more systematized study in the area of mission methods. For instance, in the nineteenth century, figures like Rufus Anderson (1796–1880), Alexander Duff (1806–1878), and Roland Allen (1868–1947) initiated a missiological debate regarding methodological approaches, and their contributions are in this area.[4] For example, Allen designed his own missionary method and transferred church authority to the young churches as a means of self-propagation and

---

1. See Skreslet, *Comprehending Mission*, 135.

2. Donovan, *Christianity Rediscovered*, 3–4. For more information regarding the missionaries doing something about slavery in Africa, see Kollman, *Evangelization of Slaves*.

3. See Schmitz and Rzepkowski, "Missionary Methods," 316–21.

4. See Schmitz and Rzepkowski, "Missionary Methods," 316–21.

self- maintenance.[5] Perhaps the first to publish a comprehensive account of missionary methods was Duff. He identified three missionary methods used in India, which is where he lived as a missionary: missionary preaching, translation and circulation of the Christian scriptures, and Christian education.[6] Anderson emphasized evangelization though self-propagation and independent local churches.[7]

Moreover, according to Josef Schmitz and Horzt Rzepkowski, at the 1910 World Missionary Conference in Edinburgh, the question of missionary methods played an important role. For the immense missionary activity throughout the whole world, it was necessary to design a methodological, strategic, and tactical approach. In this conference, it was emphasized that each country needed and had the right to its own missionary method and tactical approach.[8] Nevertheless, in the actual implementation of mission, the participants realized that there were activities common to all: proclaiming the gospel, founding and organizing communities, and distributing the Bible. Furthermore, the legacy of Edinburgh 1910 and its impact on subsequent missionary practice were in seven areas: the geographic division of the world into Christian and non-Christian, the concept of race and culture, the pursuit of church unity, the role of women in mission, missionary study and training, cooperation among mission organizations, and ecumenical unity.[9]

In the early twentieth century, Roman Catholics had their debates over missionary strategy. The key question addressed in Protestant circles was around the value of civilizing activities to mission. On the other hand, Catholic strategists focused on two schools of thought.[10] The Louvain school emphasized the need to extend the visible structures of the institutional church.[11] "The aim of mission, according to this way of thinking, was to plant new communities of faith in places where the church did not

---

5. For more on Roland Allen's missionary methods, see Allen, *Missionary Methods: God's Plan*, 3–11; Roland Allen, *Missionary Methods: St. Paul's*.

6. See Emmott, "Alexander Duff," 167.

7. Beaver, "Legacy of Rufus Anderson," 94–97.

8. See Stanley, "World Missionary Conference," 17–18. See also Stanley, *World Missionary Conference*.

9. Phan, "World Missionary Conference," 105.

10. See Skreslet, *Comprehending Mission*, 139.

11. Pierre Charles (1883–1954), a priest of the Society of Jesus, is recognized as the leading theoretician of the Louvain school. See Joseph Masson, "Legacy of Pierre Charles," 118–20.

already exist and to replicate the organizational structures of settled church life as quickly as possible."[12] The alternative view was offered by the Münster school, which "stressed the importance of gospel proclamation (even to nominal Christians) and the conversion of individuals."[13]

As mentioned previously, Roman Catholic research and discussion on missionary methods are not as developed as the Protestant approach. Chapter 1 showed that the Second Vatican Council not only brought a new understanding of the mission of the church but was itself a missionary council. "Mission is what gave the council its basic direction."[14] It was after the Second Vatican Council that the concept of liberation played an important role in discussions of missionary strategy among Catholic theologians.[15] Reflection on mission methods from a liberation perspective focused on problems of injustice, especially in the political and economic spheres, was keen to the mission enterprise. This meant identifying and exposing the deep causes of poverty.[16] Some helped to organize resistance toward the problem of injustice by undertaking projects of education to empower the poor. Others tried to create new social structures that reflect the reign of God proclaimed by Jesus.[17] Others included promoting gender justice, human rights, and respect for religious and cultural minorities.

Hence, it is evident that since the nineteenth and twentieth centuries, many other theologians and missiologists started to bring into conversation the development of new missionary methods and took into consideration the needs and culture of specific societies by using more interdisciplinary resources. The following will use the insights of Bevans's article "Seeing Mission through Images" to illustrate some approaches to do mission/ministry work in different contexts.[18] In the article, Bevans reflects on eight images of missionaries. His intention is to bring an understanding of what mission entails in light of the challenges and concerns of more recent times.

---

12. Skreslet, *Comprehending Mission*, 139.

13. Skreslet, *Comprehending Mission*, 139. The view offered by the Münster school is often linked to Joseph Schmidlin (1876–1944). See Müller, "Legacy of Joseph Schmidlin," 109–13.

14. Bevans and Gros, *Evangelization and Religious Freedom*, 3.

15. Skreslet, *Comprehending Mission*, 140.

16. See Gutiérrez, *Theology of Liberation*, 3–9.

17. See Costas, *Christ outside the Gate*, 21–42.

18. Bevans, "Seeing Mission through Images," 158–69.

Toward a New, Praxis-Oriented Missiology

The first image presented is the treasure hunter. Missionaries/ministers do not come to a country or culture with something to sell, but they have something precious to offer (the gospel). The function of the missionary/minister is to look for the treasure which is already unearthed in the culture. In order to find the hidden treasure, the missionary/minister must dig into the soil of a new culture. The good news is not a detailed description of what the treasure is but rather a declaration of that treasure. Moreover, missionaries/ministers come to a new culture confident to find the treasure they already have found in their own culture.

The second image is the teacher. The missionary/minister comes with the attitude that he or she knows what needs to be known and that the students know nothing. Here Bevans uses Freire's banking method as an analogy. Bevans shows that contrary to the banking method concept, a good teacher is the one who learns from the students, never ceases to be a learner, and is a companion on the way to wisdom.[19]

The third image is the prophet. The missionary/minister speaks the word of God to people and denounces the unjust structures that make genuine human existence impossible.

The fourth image is the guest. Missionaries/ministers are not in their own lands and cultures. One must cultivate an attitude of being a guest and avoid an arrogant approach. The missionaries/ministers must appreciate the hospitality the host can provide, recognizing that they have no real rights before their hosts. One basic attitude missionaries/ministers must cultivate as part of their missionary activity and spirituality is that of being a guest.

The fifth image is the stranger. The missionaries/ministers are strangers in two senses: (1) In the other culture or country, that culture or country will always be "other" to the missionary/minister. (2) Missionaries/ministers become strangers in all cultures, including their own. When they return to their own culture, they do not return the same.

---

19. Freire's concept of banking education illustrates the rooted mechanisms of perpetuating unjust structures and when education becomes an instrument of oppression. Banking education is understood as an act of depositing in which the students are the depositories and the teachers are the depositors. The more passive the students are, the more they will adapt to society's thinking. Banking education minimizes or annuls the student's creative power and stimulates their credulity, which serves the interest of the oppressor and becomes the perfect condition for the student to see the oppressor as generous subjects. When the subject does not fight for his/her own interest or cultural and social emancipation, the power of transforming this world is shut down. Hence, for Freire, it is important to understand that to teach is to create possibilities and not just the transferring of knowledge. See Freire, *Pedagogy of the Oppressed*, 72–79.

The sixth image is the partner where ministry is often conceived as doing things for others. In actuality, the job of the missionary/minister is not to do everything or to be a leader of everything but to call every member to partnership in ministry.

The seventh image is the migrant worker. Just as migrant workers must go where the job is, so the missionaries/ministers might see themselves as workers who must go where the local church has a need.

The last image is the ghost. Missionaries/ministers often do not get credit for the work they do and often feel nameless because they move on and leave behind the work they started.

These eight images mirror some challenges of mission methods. One can see the need for constant adaptation, listening to the signs of the times, and consequently more contextualized mission methods.[20] Sadly, the use of some methods with a very classical and westernized approach that is culturally insensitive still exist in the twenty-first century. One can also see that the growing identity of local churches is a reality that is important to take into account in the mission enterprise. As Louis Luzbetak expresses, it is necessary to give voice and listen to the needs of the local church.[21] Lastly, these images show how religion makes sense within a particular culture. Therefore, the role of culture and the interaction of the human being in specific cultures is taken more seriously when doing mission/ministry work.

I would like to conclude this section with Luzbetak's Catholic perspective on missionary methods.[22] Luzbetak reflects that in the two thousand years of mission action, certain missionary methods like ethnocentrism and accommodation have led to some controversies.[23] In missionary methods, enculturation (the process from learning a culture from one's society) is a necessary process to reach contextualization, but there is the danger to turn it into ethnocentrism. Ethnocentrism is the tendency to over esteem the ways and values of one's own society as the

---

20. See Bevans, *Models of Contextual Theology*, 3–15.

21. See Luzbetak, *Church and Cultures*, 71.

22. My reason for using Luzbetak's perspective on missionary methods is because his work on culture had offered missiological insights for contextualizing the gospel and for constructing meaningful local theologies, aspects of which have significant resonance in Bevans's and Freire's work. For Luzbetak, culture is the backbone in contextualizing theology. He portrays contextualization in a similar way as incarnation and inculturation, which will be explained in this section.

23. Luzbetak, *Church and Cultures*, 64.

Toward a New, Praxis-Oriented Missiology

normal, right, proper, and best way of doing things.[24] According to Luzbetak, there are three common forms of ethnocentrism: (1) paternalism, (2) triumphalism, and (3) racism.[25]

Missionary accommodation is as old as the church itself. Accommodation is the term used for the trials to adapt and assimilate the good news to every culture.[26] One of the misappropriations of accommodation (and of enculturation and adaptation) is that they can stay in a simple tactical strategy to make contact with others easier but not incarnating the gospel message with the local culture.[27] Missionary accommodation implies that the missionaries/ministers are not in their own lands and cultures; therefore, they should be respectful to their hosts by realizing that they have no preferred rights.[28] However, Luzbetak considers that "without accommodation, the next step, contextualization, would have been considerably more difficult, if not impossible."[29]

Luzbetak understands contextualization "as the various processes by which a local church integrates the gospel message (the 'text') with its local culture (the 'context'). . . . Contextualization is also known as 'inculturation' and 'incarnation.'"[30] It involves the integrative processes by which the local church integrates the gospel with its understanding of its culture. Therefore, the elements that expose the fundamental differences between incarnation

---

24. Luzbetak, *Church and Cultures*, 65.

25. Paternalism is a misguided compassion that tends to humiliate the would-be beneficiaries, making them even more dependent on the would-be benefactor than they were before. Triumphalism is the conviction of the sending church that it has been so successful and so blessed that it now has a manifest destiny to share with the receiving church not only its faith but, more importantly, pure qualities of that faith. Racism is when the color of the skin somehow condemns certain "less fortunate" individuals to second-class citizenship not only in society at large but sometimes in church as well. Luzbetak, *Church and Cultures*, 67.

26. Luzbetak, *Church and Cultures*, 68.

27. Luzbetak, *Church and Cultures*, 68.

28. During the process of missionary accommodation, if the missionary/minister remains as a guest, the missionary/minister portrays a colonial attitude of going to a place. Instead of gratefully trying to enculturate the gospel and appreciate the values of the culture, the missionary/minister accommodates. There are cases where the missionaries/ministers can abuse the hosts' hospitality. This has been the case especially in many indigenous missions.

29. Luzbetak, *Church and Cultures*, 69.

30. It is important not to confuse the missiological term *inculturation* with the older anthropological terms of *enculturation* and *acculturation*. Luzbetak, *Church and Cultures*, 69.

and accommodation can be summed up as follows: (1) The primary agents for incarnating the gospel are the local Christian community and the Holy Spirit. (2) The direct concern of mission is to proclaim the reign of God and salvation. (3) The ultimate goal of incarnating the gospel is mutual richness. (4) The depth of cultural penetration and identification with the gospel is greater in contextualization than in accommodation.

We have seen that both Catholic and Protestant missiologists and theologians have questioned the way we do mission and continue to search for better and more appropriate ways of doing mission in different societies, contexts, and cultures. For example, nowadays there are new models of mission with a new understanding of person, culture, and society. There are also new attitudes toward religious freedom and therefore a new ecumenical awareness. It is necessary to seek the appropriate means so that the gospel can be incarnated in every culture, not with imposition but rather with respect and dialogue. Moreover, there has been an increasing awareness of making use of other academic disciplines (anthropology, sociology, psychology, ethnography, etc.) so that mission praxis can be more critically and theologically appropriate. In other words, "the" methodology for mission praxis does not exist. It is simply important to be continuously aware of the concrete needs and movements of specific societies and cultures. We need to constantly seek tactical approaches that do not lower the value of the person and culture but instead empowers the essence of the human being through the message of the gospel.

TRANSMISSION OF CHRISTIAN FAITH

The content in this section will be from a Roman Catholic perspective but not limited to it. The transmission of faith can be approached from different angles. The approach this section will offer is limited to the experiential aspect of it. It will point out that one of the main components of Christian mission is the transmission of Christian faith, which is to proclaim the good news of the reign of God and to do this through witnessing, working for social justice, and other expressions of the reign of God.[31]

---

31. When referring to the kingdom of God, I will use the symbol of the reign of God instead. The symbol of the kingdom of God is ambiguous and critiqued in our time by scholars promoting gender justice and respect for religious and cultural minorities. For example, from a feminist perspective *kingdom* of God appears patriarchal. The word *reign* in Hebrew is translated *malkuth Yahweh* and in Greek is translated *basileia tou theou*. Both translations refer to an act of reigning rather than to a particular realm or domain. For further discussion on this topic, see Quitslund, "Feminist Perspective,"

Toward a New, Praxis-Oriented Missiology

Handing on the faith, or proclaiming the good news of the reign of God, was a more or less unproblematic issue because "the transmission of faith was so firmly integrated in the general process of community social and cultural values that it was often not even necessary for the Church to provide separate instruction"[32] However, this situation has dramatically changed. Handing on the faith has become critical to the point that what could be at stake is the church's survival since she cannot live without tradition. Correspondingly, Christian faith "cannot simply be conserved and passed on under lock and key, like some valuable museum piece . . . our testimony must be new and different in a new social situation."[33] Therefore, passing on faith is not a matter of verbal formulations or cognitive learning. Women and men seek to experience faith as offering something that is relevant for their lives. For faith to be alive, it must be experienced in practice.

The transmission of Christian faith must be nurtured and arise from the "bone marrow" of the people and not engage the mind alone. For this, the transmission of faith requires appropriate means not only to unfold the message to be transmitted but for the recipient to also unfold the message received. The following will present a perspective on the experiential approach offered in some Catholic Church documents and in Thomas H. Groome's work.[34]

Faith is not simply a summary of doctrines that have been passed down to be believed. It can make us capable of an experiential assimilation of the good news about the reign of God. The foundation of faith is itself experience.[35] Throughout the centuries, this experiential side of faith has been transmitted by people such as Abraham, Job, the prophets, Jesus, Mary Magdalene, Paul, Perpetua and Felicity, or in more recent times, Mother Teresa, Gandhi, Martin Luther King Jr., Oscar Romero, Dorothy

---

134–39; Isasi-Díaz, *La Lucha Continues*.

32. Greinacher and Elizondo, *Transmission of Christian Faith*, ix.

33. Greinacher and Elizondo, *Transmission of Christian Faith*, ix.

34. My reason for using Thomas H. Groome's work in this section on the transmission of faith is because he uses critical pedagogy on Christian religious education. In Christian circles, religious education is one of the main venues to transmit faith. Groome is a professor in the Department of Theology and in the Institute of Religious Education and Pastoral Ministry at Boston College. He is a prominent Christian religious educator. Groome is best known for his "shared Christian praxis" and "sharing faith" approach to religious education. He is also recognized for making significant contributions to practical theology.

35. See Fowler, "Gradual Introduction into the Faith," 47–53.

Day, and Pope Francis, to mention a few. "The existential *in*tensity with which faith is personally adopted can only be increased at the cost of the *ex*tension of the subject matter of the faith that is passed on."[36] The subject matter of faith has the potential for solving human questions and problems of believers from yesterday, today, and tomorrow. "The interpretation of faith which has been passed down to us did not descend from heaven at some point or other, finished and complete. It was worked out, prayed for, suffered. It is the testimony of shared experiences of faith and the expression of historically moulded answers to historically moulded questions."[37] Because of this historical moulded-ness, faith can always be experiential and actual. Pope Francis, in his encyclical letter *Lumen Fidei*, says,

> The transmission of the faith not only brings light to men and women in every place; it travels through time, passing from one generation to another. Because faith is born of an encounter which takes place in history and lights up our journey through time, it must be passed on in every age. It is through an unbroken chain of witnesses that we come to see the face of Jesus.[38]

Furthermore, it is also important to take into account that the theological truths or content of faith is amazingly genuine and understandable to every society in whatever part of the world. Transmission of faith is not bound to any specific culture or institution; however, it entails being inculturated.[39] Therefore, it is important to become sensitive to the diverse forms of believing in particular social contexts.

The document *The New Evangelization for the Transmission of the Christian Faith* advocates that the Christian faith impacts the whole being

---

36. Bitter, "What Faith Shall We Hand On?," 40.
37. Bitter, "What Faith Shall We Hand On?," 40.
38. *Lumen Fidei*, no. 38.
39. Because inculturation can be understood in a variety of ways, I will render a brief explanation of what inculturation means for this paper. Aylward Shorter defines inculturation as the ongoing dialogue between faith and culture or cultures. It is a creative and dynamic relationship between the Christian message and culture and cultures. Shorter offers an approach to inculturation "from below," starting from the particular churches. For example, the Catholic Church is more aware that her pluralistic, multicultural, and multidenominational realities require new future perspectives of inculturation. Thus, Shorter would imagine a multicultural church in which local solutions to pastoral problems and local formulations of doctrine and worship are favored, and where pastoral priorities should be decided locally. This is what he means by inculturation from below or from the particular churches. See Shorter, *Theology of Inculturation*, 10, 251–53.

Toward a New, Praxis-Oriented Missiology

of a person because it is about a personal encounter, a relationship with Jesus Christ, and a response to the gift of love.

> Transmitting the faith means to create in every place and time the conditions for this personal encounter of individuals with Jesus Christ. The faith-encounter with the person of Jesus Christ is a relationship with him, "remembering him" (in the Eucharist) and, through the grace of the Spirit, having in us the mind of Jesus Christ.... "Being Christian is not the result of an ethical choice or a lofty idea, but the encounter with an event, a person, which gives life a new horizon and a decisive direction.... Since God has first loved us (cf. 1 Jn 4:10), love is now no longer a mere 'command'; it is the response to the gift of love with which God draws near to us." The Church realizes herself precisely from carrying out her task of proclaiming the Gospel and transmitting the Christian faith.[40]

Transmitting the faith is not accomplished by words alone; it requires a relationship through prayer with God, which is faith in action. In his address to members of the Pontifical Commission for Latin America, Pope Francis expressed that there is an educational emergency with regard to the transmission of the faith. An education that is "not only about imparting knowledge and transmitting content. It involves multiple dimensions: the transmission of content, habits and a sense of values."[41] Additionally, because of the many layers that it entails, the transmission of faith is a composite and not a static process: "The transmission of the faith is a very complex, dynamic process which totally involves the faith of Christians and the life of the Church. What is not believed or lived cannot be transmitted."[42] Transmitting the faith is not a task assigned to a specialized group of people or specially designated individuals; it is an experience of every Christian and the entire church.

Groome's work will complete this section. He developed a "shared Christian praxis" approach that emphasizes a paradigmatic shift toward educating the whole being of a person in Christian faith.[43] For him, Chris-

---

40. Synod of Bishops, "New Evangelization," no. 11.
41. Francis, address to the Pontifical Commission for Latin America.
42. Synod of Bishops, "New Evangelization," 12.
43. Shared Christian praxis is a participative and dialogical pedagogy in which people reflect critically on their own historical agency in time and place and on their sociocultural reality, have access together to Christian Story/Vision, and personally appropriate it in community with the creative intent of renewed praxis in Christian faith toward God's reign for all creation. Groome, *Sharing Faith*, 135.

Conscientização Enhances Prophetic Dialogue and Vice Versa

tian faith goes beyond "people's ways of 'knowing' to embrace ontology and people's whole way of 'being' as human beings in the world."[44] He argues that critical rationality should be a constructive dimension of the processes used to bring people to know their faith.

> The nature and purposes of Christian religious education require that we promote personal cognition as a critical reflective, dialectical and dialogical process that encourages a right relationship between knower and known in a community of discourse and that we broaden our concern beyond simply cognition. The incarnational principle that stands at the heart of Christianity demands a pedagogy that is grounded in and shapes people's ontic selves—their identity and agency in the world.[45]

This quote exposes the intentionality and understanding of Groome's approach to Christian religious education using critical pedagogy.[46] Groome

---

44. Groome, *Sharing Faith*, 7. Groome uses ontology more in a Heideggerian sense of "being" ourselves as we exist in relationship with historical reality. Ontology was revived by the existentialists, especially by Heidegger. For him, ontology means the study of the *being* who can reflect on and question their own being in the world.

45. Groome, *Sharing Faith*, 8.

46. Critical pedagogy stresses the need (for teachers and students) to actively transform knowledge rather than simply consume it. It is important to connect classroom knowledge to the experiences, stories, and resources that the students bring to the educational setting. Furthermore, it tries to link that knowledge with the students' capacities to be critical agents who respond to moral and political problems of their time and who see the importance of organized collective struggles. Critical pedagogy aims at enabling rather than subverting a democratic culture. Another important aspect of critical pedagogy is that it proposes a close link between theory and practice as well as reflection and action. Theory is a resource that enables us to both define and respond to problems as they surface in particular contexts. Its transformative power resides in the possibility of enabling forms of agency, not in the ability to solve problems. Its politics are linked to the ability to imagine a different world and then act differently. Critical pedagogy must be seen as a political and moral project and not a technique. It takes the relationship between how we learn and how we act as individuals and social agents seriously. In summary, there is no critical pedagogy without critical thinking. Critical thinking is an important tool for self-determination and engagement of the world. The following elements are to be considered when talking about pedagogy: (1) Education is not just limited to a school or a classroom. It has a deep social repercussion. (2) Pedagogy cannot be reduced to a series of techniques, practices, or methods. It is an ongoing project in helping all men and women to unfold their human capacities and uniqueness, which have social, political, and moral consequences. (3) It seeks a link between theory and practice as well as reflection and action. (4) Lastly, when describing critical pedagogy, it is impossible to ignore the aspect of self-transformation and participation in transforming our societies and the world. See McLaren, *Life in Schools*, 186; Giroux, *On Critical Pedagogy*, 154–71;

proposes a threefold purpose of Christian religious education: (1) the reign of God, (2) lived Christian faith, and (3) the wholeness of human freedom that is fullness of life for all. For the purpose of this section, only Groome's insights offered for a lived Christian faith will be discussed.[47]

To live out the Christian faith, Groome identifies a threefold dynamic: believing, trusting, and doing God's will. *Believing* encompasses the cognitive/mental dimension. The believing activity reflects conviction and decision. *Trusting* is the affective/relational dimension. This trusting in one's relationship with God is nurtured and realized in relationship with a Christian faith community and thus shapes our relationship with all humankind. *Doing God's will* is the behavioral/obedience dimension. It is an activity of doing God's will in the world. The importance of highlighting this threefold dynamic is to emphasize the holistic process that happens within the person who is living the Christian faith with a critical lens. The ontological element finds its expression in this holistic process since believing, trusting, and doing God's will are not just a matter of knowing. Therefore, for the appropriation of faith, using critical rationality is essential.

Groome sees the transmission of faith as an ontological enterprise. For him, this ontological turn requires a shift in how to perceive the relevance of the Christian faith, how to perceive the intended learning and outcome, and how to structure its instruction. Consequently, Groome introduces the term *conation* as a more adequate term than cognition. His understanding of conation emerges from "the recognition that we humans have a fundamental eros that moves us to realize our own 'being' in relationship with others and the world. This 'will to being' prompts us to exercise our sensate, cognitive, affective, and volitional capacities to place and to maintain ourselves as agent-subjects in relationship."[48] For Groome, conation is synonymous with the biblical understanding of *wisdom*. Here, wisdom is typically translated as heart and reflects the totally of the person: center of affections, intellectual source, the seat of volition, and conscience. Therefore, conation/wisdom is an activity of the whole person and pertains to their whole being. Conation "emerges and is realized as the whole ontic 'being' of agent-subjects actively engaged in partnership with others to

---

Barroso Tristan, "Giroux."

47. For Groome's complete development on the threefold purpose of Christian religious education, see Groome, *Sharing Faith*, 14–25.

48. Groome, *Sharing Faith*, 29.

consciously know, desire, choose and responsibly do what is most humanizing and life-giving for all."[49]

When teaching the content of faith, Groome is mindful of some important elements to achieve: (1) engage the being of people in their self-identity as agents-subjects in relationship, (2) engage the place in which the being of people is realized, (3) engage the being of people in time and the faith tradition of the Christian community over time, (4) engage people's dynamic structure for conation, and (5) engage people in decision for their truth in Christian faith.

In summary, this experiential and ontological enterprise in the transmission of Christian faith is at times the most neglected aspect regarding religious education, pastoral ministry, and missionary work. One could agree that not all pedagogies or tactical approaches develop the ontological dimension of the person. Thus, this ontological shift is an important one in the transmission of faith, let alone for the church's mission.

BEVANS AND FREIRE

The previous sections offered a general perspective regarding mission methods and the experiential aspect of the transmission of Christian faith. This section will put into dialogue Bevans's understanding of mission as prophetic dialogue and Freire's concept of *conscientização*. Then the following section will present some common elements in prophetic dialogue and *conscientização*. Recall that prophetic dialogue is not just one more approach for understanding the "why" of mission. Prophetic dialogue also contains a pedagogical approach of "how" to do mission. It is in the pedagogical implications of Bevans's thought where Freire's work intersects and where they both can enhance each other.

Generally, the most challenging aspect of the transmission of Christian faith is not knowledge but the dimension of faith that is experiential and transformative, as we have seen previously. Likewise, mission is not simply a quest for orthodoxy. The good news of the reign of God must touch the heart, mind, and will of the person in order to be expressed and lived out. It is obvious that not whatever tactical approach reaches this. We can teach and preach about justice, love, and compassion, but *to be* just, loving, and compassionate is far more challenging. So one of the riches in Bevans's and Freire's thought is that they do not stay in the cognitive

---

49. Groome, *Sharing Faith*, 30.

Toward a New, Praxis-Oriented Missiology

dimension but reach for questions of existential importance that lead to transformation: Who am I and how can I change the world?

The ministerial example of the Good Friday service provided in the first chapter will illustrate where Freire's pedagogy and Bevans's missiology intersect. The purpose is to rescue the process that makes the missionary approach or transmission of faith not something static but dynamic, alive, actual, and with a vision toward the future.

The Good Friday service was not about a theological teaching of the meaning of the cross. Nevertheless, notice how the example begins and ends with the human experience of the parishioners and the ministers and their mutual transformation and liberation. The focus will be on this mutual process of transformation and liberation. The following will depict three important aspects where prophetic dialogue and *conscientização* enhance each other.

(1) The Good Friday service intended to be a safe space for healing, consolation, and reconciliation for all those people who, due to their legal situation, were unable to be present at the funeral of their loved ones who passed away in their native country. The ministers were sensitive to the reality that many immigrants carry the heavy burden of not being able to say goodbye, forgive, or simply express feelings to their family members who have passed away. Since both ministers were dealing with a grief process like many immigrant people, they were now aware of this reality with different eyes. The personal context of the ministers and the context of the people were intersecting and offering a new reading of reality and of the content of faith.

Two aspects are worth emphasizing. (a) The process of deep listening is where prophetic dialogue and *conscientização* were intersecting and pedagogically complementing each other. Additionally, deep listening was the starting point of unfolding a process in the people and the ministers. The service intended to offer a setting to make contact, name, and express unresolved feelings so that everybody could experience reconciliation with themselves and experience a closure in their relationships, especially with the ones who had died. The deep listening process began to acknowledge a very specific suffering of the people within a very specific political context (*las redadas*). Helping the people name and be in touch with their specific suffering (each person shared their unfinished closures with the pastor) was the basis of a healing process. We did not offer psychotherapy to help the people but sparked a process of *conscientização* to help them become

Conscientização Enhances Prophetic Dialogue and Vice Versa

aware of their own suffering. Freire's process of *conscientização* is a process in understanding oneself and the other. This understanding becomes the key to transforming, reordering, and reconciling relationships. *Conscientização* leads us to understand and undergo a process of awareness within our own particular reality and context. Simultaneously, prophetic dialogue invited us to a deep listening of the context and the gospel. So prophetic dialogue and *conscientização* do not depart from a counterfeit or ideal reality. This is a key element in the transmission of faith. Moreover, prophetic dialogue and *conscientização* offered a dynamic and non-static transmission of faith. This constant listening to reality and context is what makes it dynamic.

(b) The mutual learning process (from ministers and people/teachers and students) is key for prophetic dialogue and *conscientização*. One of the most common approaches to ministerial experiences is that the minister knows everything and has something to teach the people because they do not know (remember the teacher image presented earlier). Without the awareness and humility of wanting to learn from each other, prophetic dialogue and *conscientização* would not take place. Bevans and Freire are trying to rescue this element in their approaches because a mutual learning process contains an inherent wisdom and leaves room for an experiential practice.

(2) Prophetic dialogue offers us a sense that mission needs to be approached with profound openness, presence, and respect for the other. Similarly, the process of *conscientização* allows one not only to encounter the other where they are, respecting the uniqueness of every person, culture, church, and society, but also to be constant learners. Prophetic dialogue and *conscientização* could not take place without dialogue: a dialogue with a horizontal relationship between persons, a dialogue that recognizes that everyone has something to impart and something to learn. Chapters 1 and 2 showed that not any kind of dialogue can initiate a process of transformation. For Freire, dialogue is an essential tool to help the person become a subject and not an object, and it cannot exist without humility. For Bevans, dialogue helps us approach mission with bare feet and should be done in vulnerability and in humility. This dialogical approach is the master key for a pedagogical tool for any mission endeavor. We will look at it closely by again referring to the Good Friday service.

The Good Friday service also led the ministers to acknowledge and listen to the personal human experience they were experiencing. Due to their own grieving, the ministers were facing new questions that needed new

Toward a New, Praxis-Oriented Missiology

answers about God, faith, and eschatological hope to continue ministering. The ministers were part of the same process as the people: they were vulnerable, not having all the answers to suffering and fully integrated faith in God. Prophetic dialogue and *conscientização* enhance each other in this process of seeking an authentic dialogue with the people and the particular context. The best missionary method or strategy is not having all the answers. Only a dialogue that encompasses respect, openness, willingness to learn, attentiveness, vulnerability, hospitality, humility, and honesty leads to perceive a particular context/situation in a new way and to be creative to continue re-creating our society. Moreover, the kind of dialogue that prophetic dialogue and *conscientização* proposes spurs on not only an individual but also a collective process. We can see this in the end result of the whole experience of the Good Friday service. Not only were the people able to perceive differently the meaning of the cross for their lives but also were the ministers. It was an individual and a communal experience.

(3) The Good Friday service was such a healing experience for many immigrants not because of the perfect techniques and methods applied at the service. As mentioned before, the example begins and ends with the human experience of the parishioners and the ministers and their mutual transformation and liberation. Therefore, this last point emphasizes that prophetic dialogue and *conscientização* are not two good methods or techniques that guarantee a successful result in any ministerial setting. What it is fascinating in Bevans's and Freire's thought is that both emphasize the process (of liberation, transformation, or making visible the reign of God) that continuously unfolds (or not unfolds at all) in the person and in specific contexts. The ministers were not teaching a meaning of the cross that they had theologically mastered but were finding a new meaning of the cross in a very particular way together with the people. The value of prophetic dialogue and *conscientização* has nothing to do with mastering techniques to guarantee a "successful" mission approach, but they lead us to be completely open, alert, and attentive to the present time to continue incarnating the good news of the reign of God.

Also, prophetic dialogue and *conscientização* preserve the experiential aspect of the transmission of faith. In the example, the focus was on a specific experience of suffering and the meaning of the cross in relationship with their personal reality and context. For Freire, it was very important to relate the content with the reality of the people so that knowledge could be assimilated. Similarly, Bevans's approach to mission is not about orthodoxy but to encounter the other where they are, respecting the uniqueness of every person, culture, church, and society, and recognizing that the presence of God and the Spirit is already there. Lastly, it is clear that Bevans and Freire are not proposing specific methods. On the contrary, Bevans says that *prophetic dialogue is more a habitus or spiritual discipline than anything else.* Freire also was against importing or exporting his pedagogical practices because of the danger of wanting to reproduce a technique or method. The invitation is to be more attentive to the process that could support or help the people to initiate a process of liberation or transformation. No method guarantees this; we can just learn to be active participants and respectful vessels of this process.

In summary, prophetic dialogue and *conscientização* are not methods or techniques but two different processes that complement and enhance each other, helping us to take into account the present reality of the people and the present context.

(1) Prophetic dialogue and *conscientização* preserve the experiential aspect of the transmission of faith because they do not stay in the cognitive dimension. (2) Both concepts emphasize the process of liberation and transformation that continuously unfolds in the person and in specific contexts. (3) Both propose a dynamic and non-static transmission of faith through constant listening and actualization by the people and in different contexts. (4) Prophetic dialogue and *conscientização* cannot take place without an authentic and horizontal dialogue that leads to a personal and collective experience.

(5) Both concepts have nothing to do with mastering techniques to guarantee a successful mission approach, but they help us to be more open, alert, and attentive to the present time to continue incarnating the gospel. (6) Lastly, both support a mutual learning process, one open to constant learning.

COMMON ASPECTS IN BEVANS'S AND FREIRE'S THOUGHT

Table 3.1 compares common elements in prophetic dialogue and *conscientização*.

Toward a New, Praxis-Oriented Missiology

Table 3.1. Common elements in prophetic dialogue and *conscientização*

Conscientização	Prophetic Dialogue
It is not about transferring knowledge	Mission is not transferring content
Joins theory and practice (praxis)	Incarnated activity in the witness of an individual, community, or institution
Process of *conscientização* is based on dialogue	Dialogue is more of an attitude, a *habitus*, or spiritual discipline than anything else
Respect of the autonomy, dignity, and identity of the human being	Acknowledges the importance and dignity of the human being and cultures
Awareness of our unfinishedness: The world is not finished and is always in the process of becoming	Encompasses respect, openness, willingness to learn, attentiveness, vulnerability, and humility and leads us to perceive a particular context in a new way
Process through which human beings achieve a deepened awareness of both the sociocultural reality that shapes their lives and their capacity to transform that reality	Takes into account human experience, culture, social location, and historical situation, without which social change will not take place
Importance of otherness: Liberation is in fellowship with others, interaction with the world	An invitation to discover the Spirit's presence in movements, persons, human experience, cultures, and history
Denounces dehumanizing structures to announce a structure that will humanize	Commitment to issues of justice, peace, and the integrity of creation, proceeding with cultural and contextual sensitivity
Preferential option for the poor	Giving voice to the local context and margins
Utopia and hope are natural, possible, and necessary	Announces an eschatological hope

Looking at these initial common elements in Bevans and Freire, one could see that the process of transformation and liberation inherent in the transmission of faith is not a question of transferring content nor a one-sided effort. It is a process that requires experiential knowledge of faith, dialogue, respect, and acknowledgment of the dignity and identity of the human being, awareness that we are not perfected/finished human beings or in a perfected/finished society but are in the process of becoming, strengthening the coherence between word and action. Moreover, prophetic dialogue and *conscientização* do not impose. Rather, they give room for change, justice, and transformation. Transformation is possible because of our interaction with the world.

Although Bevans and Freire come from different social locations and contexts and with very different approaches, one can certainly see many commonalities in their thoughts. Despite the ongoing changes determined by the epochal changes in our world, Christian mission is undergoing a new birth, and it is in search of paradigms with a postmodern and ecumenical lens in our pluralistic and pluri-centric world. Structures of oppression and exploitation are being called out more than ever before, and societies seek their own cultural identity and reject Western models. New cultural identities have been born (hybridity) along with freedom of religion, a greater awareness of other faiths, and new pedagogies with the desire not only to unfold the dignity of the human being but also to adapt to and improve the world's changes. These rapid changes are pushing us to new frontiers and new ways of seeking and being clear about the essence of our faith and to adapt it and transmit it to specific realities. Prophetic dialogue and *conscientização* have such flexibility to respond to the need of different contexts and realities. Moreover, along with all these changes and new considerations, one element that will prevail is the sense of commitment to transformation and liberation because it is the core of the good news of the reign of God. It is this process that prophetic dialogue and *conscientização* try to spark and genuinely recover in every person and culture.

Figure 3.1 presents the important common elements in prophetic dialogue and *conscientização*: listening; dialogue; respect for the uniqueness of each person, culture, church, and society; and openness and mutual learning in the participative process. These elements actualize the process of personal and social transformation.

Toward a New, Praxis-Oriented Missiology

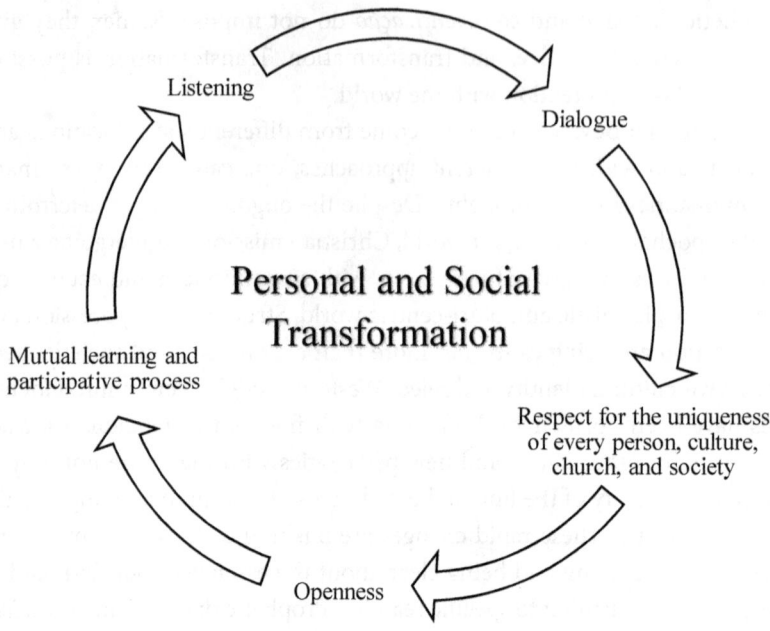

Figure 3.1. Common elements in prophetic dialogue and *conscientização*.

Finally, the common elements in Bevans's and Freire's work offer some pedagogical implications in prophetic dialogue and *conscientização* that are important to recover for the mission enterprise. (1) The process of transformation and liberation is not a question of transferring knowledge. Prophetic dialogue and *conscientização* support and enhance the development of the ontological dimension of the person. (2) For mission or ministerial experience, an embodied message is the most effective way of transmission. The gospel message requires coherence between word and action. The inherent process of prophetic dialogue and *conscientização* entails praxis. (3) Prophetic dialogue and *conscientização* are based on dialogue. Freire states that there is no freedom without dialogue. Our pluralistic and multidenominational reality requires dialogue, not whatever kind of dialogue but a prophetic one where humility can take place. (4) Prophetic dialogue and *conscientização* respect and acknowledge the dignity and identity of the human being. For a pedagogy of mission, a positive view of the human being is essential so that we can unfold the beauty and dignity of every human being because we are God's creation. (5) Prophetic dialogue and *conscientização* make us aware that we are not perfected/finished human

Conscientização Enhances Prophetic Dialogue and Vice Versa

beings but are in the process of becoming. In a pedagogy of mission, this is a central element. Without the awareness that we are in the process of becoming, it is easy to get trapped in cycles of demands and perfectionism in propagating the gospel message. (6) There is no process of prophetic dialogue and *conscientização* without the "other." In a pedagogy of mission, it is important to be able to name situations such as causes of injustice and oppression. Without *conscientização*, numbness and unawareness will thrive. (7) Freedom is lived in community and fellowship. In a pedagogy of mission, it is not a question of one's own well-being; there is a conscience of otherness/community. (8) Consequently, giving voice to the poor and marginalized, social change, justice, and transformation are possible because of our interaction with the world. (9) Lastly, in a pedagogy of mission, *hope* is necessary. It offers not only a vision to the future but a sense of acceptance of our human condition.

CONCLUDING THOUGHTS

As mentioned before, Roman Catholic research and discussion on missionary methods is not as developed as the Protestant approach. However, the increased awareness of using appropriate means so that the gospel can be incarnated in every culture and that mission praxis can be more critically and theologically appropriate is tangible. We saw how Luzbetak's approach invites us to give voice and listen to the needs of the local church. Bevans's understanding of mission as prophetic dialogue offers some important pedagogical elements to take into consideration: more humility, openness, and respect. Once again, pedagogical strategies or tactical techniques depend on and are bound to the understanding of mission.

Freire's process of *conscientização* supports a transmission of Christian faith that is experiential and ontological. It is important to nourish faith from the "bone marrow" and not engage the mind alone. This chapter also discussed Groome's proposal of using a pedagogy that develops the ontological dimension of the person when teaching and transmitting Christian faith. Furthermore, this chapter underscored the importance of using critical rationality in the processes for bringing people to know their faith. Bevans's and Freire's tactic help us to approach faith not as a sum of doctrines to be believed but to explore the capability of an experiential assimilation of the good news of the reign of God.

What prophetic dialogue and *conscientização* could offer to the mission approach and enterprise is to not seek a specific method or technique that

Toward a New, Praxis-Oriented Missiology

could produce a result but a deep listening attitude that favors the awareness and humility of wanting to learn from each other and therefore promote a mutual learning process. The key element for this approach is dialogue, a dialogue that helps us do mission or ministerial work with bare feet and vulnerability. Ultimately, prophetic dialogue and *conscientização* could initiate but not guarantee a process of liberation or transformation. However, one of the novelties of prophetic dialogue and *conscientização* is that both entail an inherent transformative and liberating process that could be unfolded. Our task is to learn to be more attentive to this process and learn to dance with the Spirit to unfold transformation to the best it could be.

The following chapter will discuss the contribution of prophetic dialogue and *conscientização* to the praxis and field of missiology in light of the contemporary Verbum Dei Missionary Fraternity vision and ministry.

4

Contribution to the Praxis and Field of Missiology in Light of Contemporary Verbum Dei Missionary Fraternity Vision and Ministry

> *El amor autentico y fuerte, igual que un enamoramiento sincero y permanente, es algo que no se improvisa ni surge espontáneamente.*
>
> *El amor a Jesús sigue la misma dinámica y crece igualmente en nosotros a medida del conocimiento vivencial que vamos teniendo de El.*[1]
>
> —JAIME BONET BONET, *ESTATUTOS VERBUM DEI*

THIS CHAPTER WILL EXPLORE the missiological implications regarding a praxis approach to the folding into of the concepts of prophetic dialogue and *conscientização*. This chapter will also demonstrate the effectiveness of prophetic dialogue and *conscientização* in my pastoral work with and among Latino immigrants in California by analyzing the spirituality and tools with which I exercise my Verbum Dei ministry. The mission of the Verbum Dei community is to empower individuals, families, and communities by leading them into a deeper relationship with God, themselves, and

---

1. My translation is as follows: "This authentic, powerful love, as in any permanent and sincere love relationship, is something not improvised or emerging spontaneously. Love for Jesus follows a dynamic and grows within us in the measure of our living knowledge of Him."

Toward a New, Praxis-Oriented Missiology

others through contemplation and partaking in the journey of Christian discipleship that is rooted in scripture.

The following will first introduce the Verbum Dei charism and mission. Second, I will present some of the diverse realities of the Latino population within my ministry. Third, I will demonstrate the effectiveness of prophetic dialogue and *conscientização* in the Verbum Dei Missionary Fraternity mission praxis. Finally, I will show how a ministry of social transformation requires a mutual process, which brings about an important missiological implication in folding into prophetic dialogue, *conscientização*, and the VDMF mission.

THE VERBUM DEI MISSIONARY FRATERNITY CHARISM AND MISSION

This section is not intended to offer an exhaustive explanation of the Verbum Dei Missionary Fraternity. After presenting general information about the community, a framework of the main elements of the VDMF charism and mission will be given in order to demonstrate how Bevans's work, Freire's work, and the VDMF charism connect.

The Verbum Dei Missionary Fraternity was founded by Rev. Fr. Jaime Bonet Bonet on January 17, 1963, in Majorca, Spain. It is an institute of consecrated life, which is contemplative-active and fully apostolic and missionary.[2] Its objective and aim is to form apostles of Christ from among people of every state of life, race, culture, and social condition for the propagation of the Kingdom of God (Matt 28:19–20).[3]

---

2. On January 17, 1963, VDMF received diocesan approval from Enciso Viana, Bishop of Mallorca, and started to live in community under the name *Misioneras diocesanas de la Palabra de Dios*. In 1969, under Bishop Alvares Lara, the Verbum Dei, with its three branches—consecrated men, consecrated women, and married couples—was named *la Fraternidad en Pía Unión*, indicating *una única familia de vida consagrada* (one single family of consecrated life). In 1993, under Cardinal Angel Suquia, Archbishop of Madrid, the branches of consecrated men and women were approved as two separate religious institutes, and the couples were approved as associates. Lastly, in 2000, VDMF received the pontifical approval by His Holiness Pope John Paul II as an *Institución de vida consagrada de la Iglesia Católica* with three branches. See Decreto of the Congregazione Per gli Istituti di Vita Consagrata e le Societá di Vita Apostolica, Prot. n. MA. 2-1/98, April 15, 2000; Decreto of the Congregazione Per gli Istituti di Vita Consagrata e le Societá di Vita Apostolica, Prot. n. MA. 2-1/98, February 27, 2012.

3. Verbum Dei Constitutions, 2012, no. 1. The original version of the VDMF Constitutions were conceived by Bonet Bonet and written with the help of some members of the community. After the pontifical approval of the community in the year 2000, the text of

Contribution to the Praxis and Field of Missiology

After his personal encounter with God at the age of fourteen, Bonet Bonet entered the minor seminary. Two years later, he was accepted in the *Colegio Mayor de Nuestra Señora de la Sapiencia*, where he became the student rector from 1950 to 1952. In 1952, Bonet Bonet was ordained by Pope Pius XII. Then, he received his first assignment as pastor in *Mancor de Valle*, a parish on the Island of Mallorca. In Mancor del Valle, while serving the sacramental needs of the people, he also began to teach people how to pray with the Word of God. It was then that Bonet Bonet generated the first apostolic movement with a group of lay women and men. He tirelessly gave retreats, which followed the model of *Cursillos de Cristiandad*. Out of the experience of prayer, preaching, and *eficacia de la Palabra* ("effectiveness of the Word" was a common expression in Bonet Bonet's preaching), men, women, and married couples began a serious discipleship. Bonet Bonet was witnessing the effectiveness of the Word in the lives of all those people whom he seriously guided and helped to persevere in their faith journey.[4]

From its origin, the VDMF has been understood by Bonet Bonet as a group "encirculating" diverse persons with profound equality: male, female, poor, rich, priest, married, single parent, religious sister, or religious brother. Bonet Bonet was convinced that the vocation to a missionary existence rests in baptism. Baptism makes us all children of God and calls us to be disciples and apostles of Christ.[5]

The VDMF describes this understanding of the founder as an ecclesial spirit, referring to the original Greek root of the term *ek-kaleo*, which means a community "called out," an assembly of persons who have been called out

---

the VDMF Constitutions was in *ad experimentum* for ten years. The 2012 Constitutions is the last version. The structure and content were modified, some of which had been made at the request of the Holy See (the ecclesiastical jurisdiction of the Catholic Church in Rome). The new modifications were made by the members of the three branches of the community, not by the founder. Therefore, the 2012 Constitutions, although trying to safeguard the founder's original writing, is the first version where the founder was not responsible for the modifications.

4. See Bonet Bonet, *Familiares de Dios*, 615; Prinz, *Endangering Hunger for God*, 181.

5. The VDMF charism came into existence alongside the Second Vatican Council. Many of the VDMF charismatic elements find resonance with the spirit of the Council. For example, both emphasize the radical equality of all the faithful by virtue of their baptism. We can see in the Dogmatic Constitution *Lumen Gentium* how the understanding of the church as People of God offers a dynamic vision where the faithful have a direct participation in the church's life and mission, and it emphasizes the personal call to holiness received through baptism. One will find the same emphasis in the VDMF Constitutions. See *Lumen Gentium*, nos. 30–38, and Verbum Dei Constitutions, 2012, nos. 2 and 65.

of their worlds to the mission. This profound conviction of Bonet Bonet is reflected in the very institutional structure of the pontifically approved *Institución de vida consagrada Fraternidad Misionera Verbum Dei*.[6]

The institutional form of the VDMF is composed of three branches: celibate women, celibate men (priest and brothers), and married couples. Each branch, although living different lifestyles and in different spaces, experiences itself in communion with the others and projects its apostolic dynamism to all persons and peoples on behalf of the Fraternity. Therefore, the VDMF is configured with a single leadership structure, formed by two branches of consecrated celibates—the female branch of "Verbum Dei missionary women" and the male branch of "Verbum Dei missionary men"—together with the branch of "Verbum Dei missionary married couples," each headed by their superiors and council members but unified by a president as the highest point person on the leadership team. The president can be a celibate women or celibate men and is elected every six years.[7]

Although ecclesiality is an important expression of the VDMF, it is important to mention that Bonet Bonet really empowered women. In fact, before the pontifical approval of the VDMF, a group of young women started living together, praying, and living out the Word of God. This was truly revolutionary for its time, since the use of the Bible was not accessible to all, especially to women.[8] He saw women as agents of evangelization with equal missionary potential to men, equally called to preach the gospel not only as a right but also as an obligation of all the baptized. In Bonet Bonet's eyes, there was no impediment for women doing retreat work, preaching, doing

---

6. Decreto of the Congregazione Per gli Istituti di Vita Consagrata e le Societá di Vita Apostolica, Prot. n. MA. 2-1/98, April 15, 2000.

7. Verbum Dei Constitutions, 2012, no. 2. The Holy See approved the three branches with the structure of one sole institute on April 15, 2000. The Holy See approved the VDMF as a New Form of Consecrated Life, or NFCL, by the Institute of Consecrated Life. The Second Vatican Council not only gave a new understanding of the church and its mission but also innovated a new understanding of consecration. The emergence of ecclesial movements brought new and renovated forms of consecrated life. The Council provided the canonical and ecclesial space for understanding consecration and consecrated life in a broader spectrum than the traditional and known context of religious life. For more information on NFCL, see Hess, "Contributions," 4–33.

8. Before the Second Vatican Council, it was expected that the pope, bishops, and priests would provide pastoral guidance on all areas of Christian living. It can be said that the hierarchy was not delivering or supporting the use of the Bible in missionary activity. The knowledge of scripture was often limited to what people heard during the liturgy and not promoted to be used by lay women and men. See Lenchak, "Function of the Bible," 3–13.

spiritual accompaniment, or even to become priests.[9] This was a radical move in Bonet Bonet's time. He was indeed a visionary regarding women's role in the church. He envisioned the capacity of women to be fully engaged in the proclamation of the Word.[10]

The VDMF is distinguished by its dedication to prayer and ministry of the Word. In the VDMF, prayer is experienced as a path to relationship and communion with God. Through this communion with God, a person is led into a process of personal integration and transformation. Hence, in the spirit of the Second Vatican Council, the VDMF is committed to all the Christian faithful, enabling them to develop their baptismal call within the church and society and empowering them to participate fully in the mission of the church in creating a world of peace, justice, equality, and dignity. This

> empowerment is centered in the spiritual life of the person: in supporting the development of the relationship with the Divine, the person integrates the diverse aspects, faculties, responsibilities, and relationships of life through a process of transformation and self-transcendence. Consequently, the person transforms and empowers the situations and circumstances, in which he or she is involved.[11]

The VDMF mission is to promote the greatest dignity for all people by empowering individuals and communities to partake in the journey of Christian discipleship. This discipleship is forged in a spirituality rooted in scripture and Catholic tradition that leads to integrating every aspect of a person's life and witnessing gospel values through our words and actions.

---

9. For Bonet Bonet, the participation in the *tria munera Christi* elevated and dignified women (and all the baptized) to priestly dignity. Since Bonet Bonet's understanding of baptism in its threefold dimension of participation in Christ was very clear, he did not doubt the possibility for women to become priest. For more information on the common priesthood of all faithful see, Congar, *Lay People*.

10. In 1966, the first VDMF women left the island of Mallorca. Bonet Bonet sent a small group to Regina Mundi, Rome, when the doors for women to study theology opened (which was a consequence of the Second Vatican Council). Another group left to begin the first mission in Peru. While some of the VDMF women were dedicated to facilitating retreats and conducting spiritual accompaniment, others were sent to study theology. Also, for first time the University of Comillas opened the doors for women in theology.

11. Prinz, *Endangering Hunger for God*, 183.

We are aware that the preaching of the living Word of God puts people in contact with Christ and that we make disciples of Christ when they "come to know" Him, follow Him and, in turn, make other disciples. Therefore, the VDMF, with the motto of the first disciples of Jesus, *orationi et ministerio verbi instantes*, and the spirit of the first Christian community, centers its specific mission in the Word of God: to pray with the Word, assimilating it until it becomes our own life, transforming ourselves in it and teaching others to do the same, so that they may pray, live and teach it experientially to others.[12]

Our apostolic activities follow the incarnational dynamic in personal prayer, preaching, witness, faith sharing, music and the arts, and in supporting individuals, families, and communities in varied social settings.

To summarize the VDMF charism, one could dare to say that VDMF spirituality focuses on increasing participation in the ongoing process of the unfolding of revelation in this world, which is a concept that is reflected in the Dogmatic Constitution on Divine Revelation *Dei Verbum*.[13] It cannot be stressed enough how revolutionary the idea of a present and ongoing revelation was in 1963. With this understanding, mission shifts to a participation in the process of the incarnation of the Word. It is noteworthy to say that when the *Dei Verbum* was budding during the Second Vatican Council prior to its promulgation in November 1965, the VDMF community was emerging in the same spirit. Bonet Bonet's primary spiritual experience at fourteen years of age and the prophetic missionary intuitions he later developed when he was a seminarian and a young priest, in a certain way, anticipated the formulation of *Dei Verbum*.[14] From a young age, Bonet Bonet's missionary zeal was clear: his purpose was to bring all people, no matter who they were or their social class, into friendship with God through a loving dialogue mediated through scripture. The following will offer parallels between Bonet Bonet's prophetic missionary intuition and *Dei Verbum*.

---

12. Verbum Dei Constitutions, 2012, no. 17. I would like to make reference to the experiential approach to Christian faith that was discussed in chapter 3. For Bonet Bonet, the Word of God, listened to, assimilated, and lived, passes on to us the same Life of God and makes us *one* with the living Word, Christ. It is in this intimate dialogue with the Word, or prayer, that our vocation and mission of preaching the gospel is rooted. The Word of God, believed and spoken and which when believed cannot but be spoken, constitutes the genuine identity of Verbum Dei. Verbum Dei Constitutions, 2012, no. 22.

13. *Dei Verbum*, no. 2; Prinz, "Hermeneutics of Hunger," 11–14.

14. Prinz, "Hermeneutics of Hunger," 12.

Contribution to the Praxis and Field of Missiology

First, the opening words of *Dei Verbum* state, "So that by hearing the message of salvation, the whole world may believe, by believing it may hope, and by hoping it may love."[15] Bonet Bonet's primary experience of intimate dialogue with God and the mission experience he had as a young priest granted him the conviction that it was crucial to build up hope in a post-war society that was flung into the Cold War and that love was connected with the person's capacity to hope and to dream to the utmost possibilities of her or his life.

Second, Bonet Bonet extended the use of the Bible to all and it contained a pastoral dimension. *Dei Verbum* was truly a revolutionary document because it added a pastoral dimension to the use of the Bible. The constitution insisted on the easy access to scripture for all Christian faithful. Scripture was offered as spiritual nourishment for all. *Dei Verbum* acknowledged the hunger for the Word of God. It also, reminded Catholics that preaching, theology, and the prayer life of the church had to be based on and nourished by the Word of God.[16] It also encouraged the scientific study of the Bible with a wider hermeneutical access to reading and understanding scripture. Additionally, more exegetical tools were available.

Third, *Dei Verbum* offers a shift in the understanding of revelation: God communicating Godself. The VDMF charism emphasizes from its origin the understanding of revelation as happening in the relationship between God and human beings instead of the two-source theory of revelation. Also, one can see in *Dei Verbum* a summary of the VDMF charism: "Through this revelation, therefore, the invisible God out of the abundance of [God's] love speaks to men [and women] as friends and lives among them, so that [God] may invite and take them into fellowship with [Godself]."[17] Julia Prinz comments, "The amazing use of the present tense in this phrase, which most probably carries Karl Rahner's signature, leads to the understanding that God continues to speak, to reveal God's self and to enter in friendship with human beings so that they can enjoy the full fellowship with God in God's abundance."[18] Revelation did not just end with the incarnation in Jesus but continues until today.

There are two more aspects worth emphasizing from the *Dei Verbum* quote just mentioned in relation to the VDMF: (a) The VDMF mission

---

15. *Dei Verbum*, no. 1.
16. See Lenchak, "Function of the Bible," 5.
17. *Dei Verbum*, no. 2.
18. Prinz, "Hermeneutics of Hunger," 11–14.

invites people into friendship with God. Participation in revelation is not just a question of knowledge of past events but rather of an ongoing friendship that leads into fellowship. (b) Bonet Bonet's notion of fellowship always had a certain connotation of social justice as well. Bonet Bonet never gave up insisting that fellowship is open to all since it is participatory, incarnational, non-exclusive, and based on the notion of the call of all the baptized. In Bonet Bonet's vision, the only needed factor for enjoying all the benefits of fellowship was a life spent in contemplative intimacy with Jesus, following him with total dedication to announce the reign of God.[19]

In summary, revelation was not completed two thousand years ago. It is an ongoing process where God and the church invite us to participate in. Therefore, the pastoral use of the Bible, which was extended with the Second Vatican Council, radically initiated a process of conversion and participation in God's revelation.

CENTRAL ELEMENTS IN VDMF MISSION

The Dynamism of the Word

This section will explain more concretely the incarnational dynamic of the Word of God, which is the core of the VDMF mission.

Bonet Bonet wrote, "*Vivir el Evangelio y convivirlo, participar de él y compartirlo y llegar a la más íntima unión con Jesús y comunión con los hermanos, es condición de vida y perfección para todos.*"[20] Bonet Bonet is expressing a relationship with the Word of God that generates a dynamism within the person, leading to an external expression or embodiment of the gospel. Also, as expressed before, the VDMF mission articulates a unique personal and intimate relationship with the Word of God. Therefore, the "method" of the VDMF mission is what the community calls the "Dynamism of the Word." The Dynamism of the Word is the core of the VDMF charism, formation, community life, and mission. This dynamism is based on *lectio divina*, but it has been adapted to the VDMF charism and its evangelizing dimension.[21] So whereas *lectio divina* follows the four steps of *lectio*

---

19. Verbum Dei Constitutions, 2012, no. 29.

20. Bonet Bonet, *Breve Ideario*. Bonet Bonet wrote this in Palma de Mallorca in 1969. My translation is as follows: "To live the Gospel, living it with others, partaking of it and sharing it, arriving at the most intimate union with Jesus and communion with our brothers (and sisters), is the condition of life and perfection for everyone."

21. *Lectio divina* is a form of prayer rooted in liturgical celebration that dates back to early monastic communities. It was a method practiced by monks in their daily

(reading), *meditatio* (meditation), *oratio* (prayer), and *contemplatio* (contemplation), the Dynamism of the Word follows listening, assimilating, living, and giving (or announcing).[22]

Prinz's diagram, the "Wheel of Metanoia," helps explain the Dynamism of the Word.[23] It is important to be aware that the Wheel of Metanoia is a tool that intends to explain a process that is, in its essence, experiential. The intention of using the diagram is not to box the Dynamism of the Word but to explain the process it contains.

---

encounter with scripture, both as they prepared for the Eucharist and as they prayed the Liturgy of the Hours. Its use continued in the Middle Ages in religious orders, such as the Benedictines and Carmelites, that not only practiced *lectio divina* daily but passed this treasure from the past on to future generations. It is a method for praying with the scriptures with a committed hearing from the depth of the heart. As one reads the scriptures, she or he invites the Word to become a transforming lens for the events of daily living and finds the presence of God more readily in the events of each day. Ezquerda Bifet, *Diccionario de la Evangelización*, 418–19; Lawlor, "Ever Ancient, Ever New."

22. To explain the prayer process in the Verbum Dei charism, we usually use the steps of *lectio divina*. For VDMF, the assimilation step is the fusion of the *meditatio* (meditation) and *oratio* (prayer) steps in *lectio divina*. Since in the VDMF community evangelization through preaching (the way VDMF understands preaching is not limited to the homiletic preaching but the sharing of faith) is an important dimension of its mission, the giving or announcing (a term also commonly used in the community as the last step of the Dynamism of the Word) is the culmination of the Dynamism of the Word because it is important that prayer leads the person to a social commitment and transformation. However, when introducing a person to Verbum Dei prayer, more than transmitting the structure of the method of prayer, the person is pedagogically induced to be in contact with the Word of God through the experience of the one who is teaching how to pray. It is easy to simply follow some steps of prayer, annulling the possibility of a transformative encounter with the Word of God.

23. Prinz, *Endangering Hunger for God*, 204.

Toward a New, Praxis-Oriented Missiology

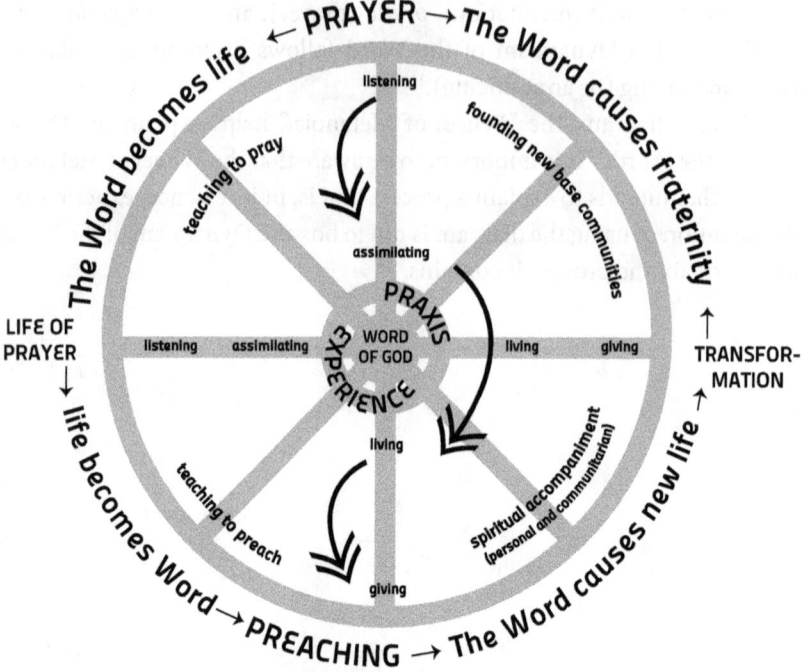

Figure 4.1. Wheel of Metanoia. From Prinz, *Endangering Hunger for God*, fig. 4.

We can see in the diagram that there are two inherent dynamics: one within the person and other one that leads to an outside expression where the Word of God becomes life in the measure the wheel turns. The Word incarnated generates new life, then the dynamism starts anew.

The wheel has in its axle the Word of God. It is where the dynamism sparks. The vertical and horizontal axioms (listening, assimilating, living, and giving) intend to reflect the inner process of the one who is in contact with the Word of God. The Dynamism of the Word starts taking place in the heart, mind, and life of the person by (1) listening to the text/scriptures and listening to one's own present reality. (2) Assimilating is the process of penetrating scripture until grasping a deeper meaning of the Word at the given moment of the person. It is not about jumping into fast conclusions and understandings of the scripture but wrestling with the text. The person confronts one's own life in the light of the scriptures leading to an inner moment of conversion. The step of assimilation is in *lectio divina* the fusion of the steps of *meditatio* and *oratio*. (3) Living is the consequence of the experience of what has been contemplated. It expresses the penetration of one's entire life with the depths of God through contact with the listened and assimilated text. At this step, the person is convicted to live out what one has contemplated from scripture and to embrace the conversion process. The step of living is in *lectio divina* the *contemplatio* step. However, the step of living is not the finale of the Dynamism of the Word. (4) The step of giving constitutes the culmination of the process. Giving or announcing (a term also commonly used in the VDMF for the last step of the Dynamism of the Word) is the result of unifying prayer with life. The interior reality of one's own assimilation has a social expression. In this last step, prayer and life are expressed in a personal and social transformation. The person is compelled to give what was received from God.[24]

The rim of the wheel (life of prayer, preaching, transformation, and prayer) needs to be understood as the driving force. It generates this constant cycle anew where, through prayer, the Word becomes life and life becomes the Word. Next, giving or announcing the Word originates new life and transformation in the person and social structures. Then, the Word engenders solidarity and fraternity. The cycle begins and ends with prayer. The Dynamism of the Word does not automatically lead from listening to giving; it implies integrative prayer and life. In other words, the Dynamism of the Word, more than a step-by-step guide to prayer, is a way of life and intends to integrate the contemplative-active life understood in the VDMF charism. Each step and movement of the Wheel of Metanoia informs, enriches, and causes the next step and movement. The dynamism is fruitful in the measure it integrates the contemplative experience with the person's diverse aspects, faculties, responsibilities, and relationships of life through a process of transformation. It reflects the prophetic expression of contemplative prayer.[25]

---

24. This last step of the Dynamism of the Word is clearly expressed in the VDMF Constitutions: "We transmit that which we have contemplated through Christ, with Him, and in Him. We communicate, proclaim and convey that which we have heard from Him, that which we have experienced, seen, tasted and known about the Word of Life." VDMF Constitutions, 2012, no. 25.

25. Some spirituality scholars have arrived at the conclusion that the contemplative life does not only mean the institutional cloistered life. For Thomas Merton, the contemplative life is a "special dimension of inner discipline and experience, a certain integrity and fullness of personal development which is compatible with a purely external, alienated, busy-busy existence." Moreover, contemplative prayer has an important role in opening up new ways and horizons not only at the personal level but also at the societal level. Therefore, it is important to recognize the prophetic and witnessing aspect

In summary, the Dynamism of the Word is not a prayer practice but a way of life. It is the process of individual and social transformation originated through the steps of listening, assimilating, living, and giving the Word.[26] The Wheel of Metanoia is representing one sole movement.[27] What this means is that one step causes the next. The process of incarnation is not complete if one of the steps is not embraced by the person. Furthermore, the spiritual life and social transformation are not separated or isolated from scripture. The key point in this dynamism is to continue spinning the wheel, which will lead to a deeper contemplation and incarnation of the Word of God.

Intimate Relationship with the Word of God[28]

As mentioned previously, the VDMF mission articulates a very unique personal and intimate relationship with the Word of God. This section will offer a brief summary of Bonet Bonet's call since it reflects the core of the VDMF charism and its very specific way of relating with the Word of God.

At the age of fourteen, Bonet Bonet had an intimate dialogue with God, which had three momentums. The first is related to Bonet Bonet's own happiness and a response to young adolescent disbelief. The second is an experience before the crucifix and Bonet Bonet's call to heal the body of Christ. The last one is the experience before the Eucharist and Bonet Bonet's understanding to continue Jesus's mission.

In the first momentum of Bonet Bonet's intimate dialogue with God, he told God, "*¡Si existes, hazme feliz!*" (If you exist, make me happy). In that dialogue, or contemplative prayer, God granted him a deep experience of happiness. He experienced himself loved and accepted to the point that he was compelled to share it with others.

The second momentum of the dialogue was Bonet Bonet's encounter with the Crucified Christ. When dialoguing with God while having a crucifix

---

of contemplative prayer. See Merton, *Contemplation*, 154–61; Louf, *School of Contemplation*, 9.

26. See Hess, "Contributions," 53–54.

27. See Prinz, *Endangering Hunger for God*, 205.

28. Bonet Bonet recently died on June 25, 2017. I had the privilege to meet our founder in person and did several spiritual exercises directed by him. What is written in this section is a very well-known story of his vocation and call transmitted orally by him in his preaching or one-on-one conversations. I was a witness of Bonet Bonet's intimate relationship with the Word of God. He tirelessly spoke of his close relationship with God and led us to have this intimacy with God.

in his hands, Bonet Bonet asked God, "*¿Qué te ha pasado?*" (What had happened to you). The response he heard in his heart was, "*Has pasado tú*" (You happened). Then, Bonet Bonet heard in his heart the words, "*Tengo sed*" (I thirst).[29] At that moment, Bonet Bonet perceived the call to heal the wounded body of Christ and to quench the thirst of God's people.

The last momentum is Bonet Bonet's dialogue with God before the Blessed Sacrament. He was trying to understand why God was hidden, powerless, and with no voice in the Eucharist. Then, he had the inner experience of understanding that Jesus was there with no hands or feet and was unable to speak. Jesus asked Bonet Bonet if he wanted to be his hands and feet and carry on Jesus's mission.

There is much theological depth to be analyzed in this single foundational faith experience of Bonet Bonet. However, the following discussion will focus on the missiological aspect, specifically the experiential aspect of faith. First, it will be helpful to emphasize some characteristics of the dialogue between God and Bonet Bonet. (1) Bonet Bonet approached God with no boundaries and with his reality of life.[30] (2) The dialogue was fully sincere. Bonet Bonet exposed to God his deepest existential questions. (3) Moreover, it was not a monologue. Bonet Bonet did not just pour onto God his questions but dared to deeply listen to God's response to his existential questions. (4) Lastly, the dialogue Bonet Bonet had with God was deeply intimate.

This dialogue led Bonet Bonet not only to know God as friend and have an experiential knowledge of God but also led him to personal and social transformation. Moreover, we saw in chapter 3 the importance of the

---

29. John 19:28.

30. Bonet Bonet's childhood was marked by the Spanish Civil War. During that time, the Catholic Church in Spain was run by the Spanish bourgeois middle class. The socialist Spanish republic came into power in 1931 and was against the bourgeois Catholic Church. During the years from 1931 to 1934, the Spanish government destroyed the privileges that the Catholic Church had since 1875. The government's primary interest was to separate the state from the Church. Consequently, one way of wanting to separate and terminate the Catholic Church was through boldly reinforcing the rigid measures of the government. The government sought to take away the church's privileges. During that time, the communist were also involved in slaughtering innocent people and church people. (Bonet Bonet used to share with us his memories of his young age when the government destroyed churches and killed priests without reason. He was deeply moved by the dead whom he had known.) Bonet Bonet, at his early age, was aware of the consequences of the Spanish Civil War, the ruthless way of governing, and the church's persecution. See Callahan, "Evangelization," 491–503; Martin Rubio, "Persecución Religiosa," 43–71; Prinz, *Endangering Hunger for God*, 187–88.

Toward a New, Praxis-Oriented Missiology

transmission of faith in a more experiential way. We can clearly see in Bonet Bonet's intimate dialogue with God what the document *The New Evangelization for the Transmission of the Christian Faith* expresses: the Christian faith affects the whole person because of a personal encounter with Jesus, an encounter with love that requires a total response.[31]

In other words, the intimate dialogue that Bonet Bonet had with God as a fourteen year old, granted him an experiential knowledge of God and of the Christian faith. This led him to a profound personal transformation and a deep commitment to Jesus Christ embodied in healing the wounded body of Christ. Bonet Bonet's experience fully embodies the Dynamism of the Word.

The VDMF charism offers the church many spiritual riches. As in the life of Bonet Bonet, one can see the positive impact in a person when he or she is open to the Dynamism of the Word and has an experiential knowledge of God. Taking a step back, it is incredible to see how Bonet Bonet's core experience of God has impacted thousands of people around the world. The VDMF, a young community with a little more than fifty years in existence, has expanded to thirty-two countries, enjoys a healthy membership, and is very vibrant. The VDMF is probably the most stable and "successful" NFCL. (The VDMF is frequently asked for advice from other NFCL). The VDMF carries and contains a freshness of faith and life that is attractive. One can agree that the life and vibrancy of the VDMF is provided by the dynamic, living, and actual experience of faith. The Dynamism of the Word leads the person to a constant conversion and transformation. Faith does not allow the person to become static and conformist. However, since the base of the VDMF charism is very experiential, one of the common tendencies and risks of the VDMF mission praxis is trying to secure a process of transformation and to develop a method that could guarantee a "successful" process of transformation. The following section will provide a perspective on a growing area in the VDMF mission with the intention of bringing awareness to the very delicate elements of a transmission of faith that is experiential.

---

31. Synod of Bishops, "New Evangelization," no. 11. Additionally, it is worthwhile to mention that Pope Paul VI's apostolic exhortation *Evangelii Nuntiandi* deeply inspired and influenced Bonet Bonet's understanding of evangelization, which supported a transmission of faith with a more experiential character. The document emphasized that the modern world needs images more than words. As such, the world needs to see witnesses of a new possible way of living in order to be introduced to the good news. This witnessing element is essential to VDMF mission praxis.

A GROWING AREA IN VDMF MISSION

As mentioned before, there are many riches that the VDMF charism can offer. However, since the base of the charism is very experiential, one of the common tendencies is to lack trust in this flexible and open-ended invitation that springs forth from every missionary move. The consequence of this tendency is to develop structures that try to control the process of the Dynamism of the Word and the intimacy with the Word of God to "guarantee" transformation in the person and therefore in society. When entering the spiritual realm, however, it is never possible to control and structure the Spirit of God.

Interestingly enough, the VDMF mission praxis identifies with the mission of the Apostle Paul:

> The Verbum Dei Missionary Fraternity wishes to manifest the spirit of the first Christian community of the twelve Apostles in their dedication to prayer and the ministry of the Word, and the tireless missionary zeal of Saint Paul in his proclamation of the Word and the formation of communities that live and announce the Gospel.[32]

Bonet Bonet indeed admired Paul's eagerness to proclaim the good news of the reign of God and his dedication to the ministry of the Word.[33] Thus, the VDMF has taken Paul's mission praxis as the example to follow.

After learning about the dialogue Bonet Bonet had with God, one could grasp that Bonet Bonet's inner fire to love God and God's people was because of his experiential knowledge of God and of faith. The inner motivation did not spark because Bonet Bonet learned from Jesus's mission in a book. Bonet Bonet deeply understood the motivation of Paul's missionary life.[34] As it is known, the Apostle Paul is one of the main missionary figures

---

32. Verbum Dei Constitutions, 2012, no. 65.

33. Following Acts 6:4, the VDMF motto is, "We will devote ourselves full-time to prayer and to the ministry of the Word."

34. Bonet Bonet had a tireless missionary zeal like Paul. This zeal came after their experiential knowledge of God in their own time and circumstances. Bonet Bonet wanted to announce the Word of God and to reach out to all women and men of every race, culture, and social class like Paul: "*Que todos lleguen al conocimeinto de la verdad, sean, se sepan, y sientan hermanos [y hermanas], hijos [e hijas] de un mismo de un mismo Padre, con los mismos derechos y deberes.*" Bonet Bonet, "Breve Ideario," 7–8. In fact, a few years after its foundation, VDMF became an international community. VDMF is currently present in thirty-two countries in five continents. Bonet Bonet was always restless about the way the gospel could be presented and announced to all, how to make disciples of

Toward a New, Praxis-Oriented Missiology

in Catholic and Protestant circles. In less than ten years, he established the church in four different provinces. The work of the apostle was and still is admirable. Many missiologists, Catholic and Protestant, are interested in understanding Paul's missionary method and pedagogy.

Before displaying a growing area in the VDMF mission praxis, some of the most relevant elements of the Pauline missionary method (which has been used in Protestant and Catholic for the praxis of mission) will be discussed with the aim of situating the reader in the Pauline method and providing a more missiological approach to the growing area for VDMF mission praxis. Material by Roland Allen and David Bosch will help introduce the Pauline missionary method.

Allen's famous book *Missionary Methods: St. Paul's or Ours?* was first published in 1912. In this book, he identifies three strategic points in Paul's mission: (1) presentation of the gospel, (2) converts, (3) and organized churches.[35] One of Allen's major contributions to missionary methods is that he advocated for the selfhood of the local churches around the world (self-supporting, self-propagating, and self-governing).[36]

However, Bosch's approach places more emphasis on the missionary dimension of Paul's theology.[37] He presents some characteristics of Paul's missionary paradigm. The first characteristic is *the church as a new community*. The four provinces that Allen emphasized in his work came into existence as a consequence of Paul's mission. These churches were in a world divided culturally, religiously, economically, and socially. In the midst of this, Paul finds it impossible to give up on the unity of the one body in spite of all differences. This strategy has a theological principle: one people have been baptized into Christ. The members of the new community find their identity in Jesus Christ rather than in race, culture, social class, or sex.[38]

Christ, and how to create faith communities. All these are some of the key elements in the Pauline missionary method.

35. Allen, *Missionary Methods: St. Paul's*, 10–17.
36. See Schmitz and Rzepkowski, "Missionary Methods," 316–21.
37. See Bosch, *Transforming Mission*, 172–81.
38. See Bosch, *Transforming Mission*, 174–75. In regards to VDMF mission, Bonet Bonet insisted, as Paul did, in the unity of the body of Christ with the principle that baptism make us one. However, Bonet Bonet's organic understanding of responding in the body of Christ (loving Christ in all) gave him the conviction that the whole world was the body of Christ. The unity of the body of Christ was beyond baptism. As a matter of fact, the world map is a more frequent centerpiece decoration of VDMF chapels, which is not just as reminder of praying for the world but to remember that world that is loved and embraced by the cross and resurrection of Christ. For Bonet Bonet, the creation

The second characteristic is *mission in the context of God's imminent triumph*. It is important to take into consideration Paul's understanding of his mission within the horizon of Christ's *parousia*. Paul, when doing mission, had the awareness that he was paving the way for God's coming triumph. Paul had his eschatological convictions: (a) He expected an ultimate resolution to the contradictions and sufferings of life in God's triumphal coming. (b) Our life as Christians is only real when it is anchored in the knowledge of God's victory. (c) Our mission in the world only makes sense if it is undertaken in the knowledge that our "accomplishments" will one day be consummated by God. With this eschatological understanding, Paul also offers a hopeful future.[39]

The third characteristic is *mission and the transformation of society*. Paul's apocalyptic vision raises the issue of the relationship between church and the world and the question whether apocalyptic eschatology has anything to say about the church's call in society. In Paul's time, there was a concrete social, political, religious, and cultural reality. Paul's ethics is not centered in knowing what is good but in knowing who the Lord is. Rather than emphasizing ethical passivity, Paul emphasizes active participation in God's redemptive will in the here and now.[40]

The last characteristic is *mission in weakness*. Paul does not present an illusory escape from suffering, weakness, and death by means of an enthusiastic proclamation that Christ won the victory. Rather, Paul's revaluation of all values has its roots in the creative tension of the Christian existence between justification already granted and guaranteed redemption.[41]

Missiologists and the VDMF community alike accept Paul's apostolic work as normative for continuing the mission of the church. The mentioned characteristics—*the church as a new community, mission in the context of God's imminent triumph, mission and the transformation of society, and mission in weakness*—resonate well with the VDMF mission praxis. Nevertheless, it is tempting to draw quick solutions and to apply Paul's missionary theology to our contemporary situation, forgetting that

---

of faith communities was the process of empowerment to enable a person to empower others. He used the term *hacer-hacer* (to make-to make). Bonet Bonet's vision was to empower a person so that that person empowers another and subsequently others. For a better understanding of the *hacer-hacer* process, we can use as a parallel term "snowball system." See Prinz, *Endangering Hunger for God*, 182.

39. See Bosch, *Transforming Mission*, 176–77.
40. See Bosch, *Transforming Mission*, 178–79.
41. See Bosch, *Transforming Mission*, 179–81.

Toward a New, Praxis-Oriented Missiology

Paul developed his missionary theology and strategy in a very specific context and epoch. If taking the Pauline missionary method as a model for mission praxis, the challenge is to defend the experiential knowledge of God and to prolong the logic of Paul's theology and mission within historical circumstances that are very different from his. It is important to also have in mind that Paul's mission praxis was a lifelong process. It took him time to realize and formulate, for example, the importance of doing *mission in weakness*. VDMF members are taught that mission in weakness is important for mission praxis, but mission in weakness is best understood through experience. Like Paul, it requires life experience to realize such an important theological insight for mission.

With all these said, the VDMF mission praxis has the constant temptation of wanting to create a method that guarantees a successful result for mission. In fact, Bonet Bonet saw this danger. He was not a pedagogue or theologian. He was a great poet. With his artistic soul and his own life, Bonet Bonet transmitted his passion for God. People were able to feel God's intimacy through what Bonet Bonet transmitted. To go against any pre-established missionary method or technique, Bonet Bonet insisted that *una vida tiene que "ser" Palabra* (a life needs "to be" the Word) as the best way to transmit the VDMF charism. Paul's mission is definitely a great example to admire and from which insightful theological elements to perform Christian mission can be drawn. However, the objective of the VDMF mission praxis is not to safeguard the transmission of the knowledge of the deposit of faith. The VDMF charism depends on the active participation of the person in one's own faith journey. What this means is that the person needs to be the agent of one's own journey. Being a missionary requires the full investment of one's own life and experience to lead the person to an experiential knowledge of God and of the Christian faith. How to keep that alive does not depend on methods.

In other words, the growing area of the VDMF mission praxis is more than focusing on insightful strategies of the Pauline method and wanting to apply them to the VDMF charism. It is important to rescue and value the process that leads to personal and social transformation by listening to the signs of the times. Every age brings new insights and challenges for mission or ministerial work. More importantly, VDMF mission requires people who are willing to be challenged by their own experience and by the experience of the world and to find ever-growing and changing ways to "be the Word" as the essence to proclaiming it.

Contribution to the Praxis and Field of Missiology

FOLDING INTO THE CONCEPTS OF PROPHETIC DIALOGUE AND *CONSCIENTIZAÇÃO*

This section will present how the concepts of prophetic dialogue and *conscientização* have helped me in my Verbum Dei pastoral work with and among Latino immigrants in California. First, I will offer a brief context of California's Latino immigrant population. The context is limited to my experience and scope of ministry. Then, I will layout Bevans's and Freire's contributions to my Verbum Dei ministry.

Today's Context of California's Latino Immigrant Population

As a religious missionary sister working in the United States, one of my ministries for more than fifteen years has been working with the Latino immigrant population: young adults, young couples, women, and married couples. There are diverse realities within the Latino population, which require a delicate process of coming to know their particular situations, culture, and their specific needs. The following describes these realities, which are based on my experience working with them.

Many of our Latino people have deep wounds and a lack of love that has impeded them from growing and flourishing humanly speaking and sometimes even spiritually. For example, some come from broken families or single-parent homes and have suffered the consequences of growing up on their own without a stable family foundation. Some come from a very abusive (physically or verbally) environment. Others work extremely hard in order to sustain their children and therefore have little contact or communication with their spouse or children. Although family is very important for Latino people, due to the above-mentioned situations, the meaning and sense of family is constantly threatened.

Many of them live every day with a high level of fear and tension of being deported because they are undocumented. This level of tension has dramatically increased with the current presidential administration. As a result of these and many other factors, people find themselves with depression and low self-esteem and have the tendency to isolate themselves for fear of being denounced.

Many of the young people who have come to the United States undocumented have a difficult time continuing onto higher education, and they conform to simple and often unjust employment. The ones that had the opportunity of finishing university studies are not able to work in their fields because they have been using inauthentic social security numbers. After so much effort, they finish working in restaurants, become Uber drivers, babysit, and so forth. Many young Latinos end up emulating models and ideals that American society presents, subsequently losing their own self-worth, values, and faith principles that they had learned in their families. Therefore, they feel ashamed by their Latino family and background. They experience severe cultural shock because they feel that they are neither Latino nor American, and they find themselves in an identity crisis.

A high percentage of Latino women have been brutally abused (physically, psychologically, sexually, and verbally) by their own father, brother, cousins, or husband or in the risky and sometimes dangerous journey of crossing the border. They are an easy target of a *machista* society, that is, one in which the role of women is to serve and please the male. The number of single mothers who must have two or three jobs in order to provide basic needs for their children is shocking. Since they are the ones providing, cooking, and attending to their children, they do not have time to take care of themselves or even see a doctor. If they get sick, they do not have the privilege to stay at home to recover. They go to work sick because they are afraid of losing their jobs and obviously because they need the money. The wages of most undocumented people are unstable. So many live day by day with the uncertainty of whether they can provide for themselves or their family.

These realities openly expose the depth of the unjust social-political structure. Regarding Latino reality (or any other recent immigrant ethnic group), it is very important not to come to rash conclusions and categorize all Latinos under the same standards. Though many can have a Latino background, the realities that immigrant Latinos live here in the United States are very different from those who live in their own country. Also, not all Latinos living in the United States are poor or uneducated.[42]

---

42. According to the United States Census Bureau, the population of Latinos living in the US in 2016 was 30,666,598. From that total, the number of males holding a bachelor degree or higher was 2,052,412, and the number of females holding a bachelor degree or higher was 2,460,713. "Educational Attainment," American Fact Finder, US Census Bureau, accessed March 9, 2018, https://factfinder.census.gov/faces/ tableservices/jsf/pages/productview.xhtml?pid=ACS_16_5YR_S1501&src=pt.

Contribution to the Praxis and Field of Missiology

Verbum Dei Ministry Applied to the Immigrant Population

How can the VDMF charism give an answer to the reality of the Latino immigrant population? Having in mind the two main elements of the VDMF mission—Dynamism of the Word and intimate relationship with the Word of God—teaching the Latino people how to pray with the Word of God and to put the Word into practice can be a great answer. This will lead them to a friendship and intimacy with God and deepen their spiritual life and thereby the living gospel message in their families and transform their surroundings.

The majority of ministries with Latino immigrants are focused on the visible and material needs of the people: immigration assistance (which embraces a wide range of activities, for example, helping them to get a driver's license, processing legal papers, studying to become US citizens, etc.), setting agencies to help them find a job, giving food to families, offering ESL classes, GED preparation, and medical services, to mention a few. All those ministries are important and necessary, but very few pay attention to the spiritual development and empowerment of the immigrant Latino population. What Verbum Dei offers them through the Dynamism of the Word and the intimate relationship with the Word of God is a liberation spirituality.[43]

---

43. Several authors have advocated that spirituality and liberation are one. That is why they call it liberation spirituality. From the decade of the 1960s, the Latin American spirituality of liberation spread. "Liberation spiritualities developed at the intersection between two givens: the experience of the oppression and God who makes [Godself] known as One who takes the side of the poor. The two dimensions are related to each other within the context of community." Waaijman, *Spirituality*, 217.

I would like to provide the reader some insights in the area of liberation spirituality offered by Gustavo Gutiérrez and Robert McAfee Brown. Gutiérrez depicts some important elements in a liberation spirituality: (1) Spirituality must establish connections between prayer and action. (2) "We all have the same vocation: to rise to life with the people in its spirituality." Gutiérrez, *We Drink*, 32. To reach this implies to change the old ways of a spirituality that generates individualism and gives room for new ways of discipleship. Gutiérrez's connection between discipleship and spirituality is clear. Discipleship is rooted in the experience of an encounter with Jesus Christ, in which the Lord takes the initiative. Such an encounter is the starting point of a spiritual journey. (3) Spirituality is a walking in freedom according to the spirit of love and life. A life according to the spirit is not in opposition to the body. It is an existence in accord with life, love, peace, justice, and against death. (4) Spirituality is the area of the Spirit's action, which is characterized by freedom. Gutiérrez, *We Drink*.

Brown presents three levels of liberation: liberation from unjust social structures, liberation from the power of fate, and liberation from personal sin and guilt. These three levels are necessary and are interrelated. McAfee Brown, *Spirituality and Liberation*.

Toward a New, Praxis-Oriented Missiology

In reality, by leading the people to experience the Dynamism of the Word, what Verbum Dei offers is a faith community where members mutually support one another to nourish and develop their faith. The faith community is centered on "the *Word*, and the *salvation* and *integral liberation* of the *whole human* person at the *individual* and *social* level. Instead of objects of the process . . . the faithful become the active subjects of their own evangelization."[44] As a community, members not only find support in their faith journey, they also become a powerful instrument of evangelization in our society today.

The process of transformation and liberation for Latino immigrants, as mentioned in chapter 2, starts with *conscientização*. This process makes it possible for people to enter the historical process as responsible subjects and assist people in self-affirmation. It is through this conscious-raising process that the poor and marginalized can be free from unjust social structures. Praying with the Word of God, people enter into this liberation and transformative process, as seen in the Wheel of Metanoia.

Moreover, a liberation spirituality brings hope. The process of liberation is reached when the person has the capacity to hope and dream that it is possible to transform first their personal lives, then the broken structures of families, and finally to question the unjust structures of society so they can be transformed.

Every ministry faces challenges. One of the big challenges when doing ministry with the Latino immigrant population is that as the oppressed they suffer from a duality: without freedom, they cannot exist authentically, but they fear freedom. They struggle for liberation, but they have internalized so much the image of the oppressor that their vision of liberation is to become the oppressor.[45] There is a big challenge to overcome this fallacy. They have internalized within them their oppression that sadly their fear paralyzes the process of transformation and liberation. It takes time and trust to overcome that fear. Freire expressed it well: "The process of liberation is a childbirth, and a painful one."[46] Liberation is not given simply by wanting it. It is not a self-achievement. It is a slow process that requires the

---

Therefore, "liberation is an all-embracing process that leaves no dimension of life untouched." Brown, *Spirituality and Liberation*, 123.

44. Azevedo, "Basic Ecclesial Communities," 644.

45. Freire saw this dualism as the most challenging aspect when working with the oppressed. See Freire, *Pedagogy of the Oppressed*, 183.

46. Freire, *Pedagogy of the Oppressed*, 49.

person's participation, the grace of God, and a mutual process where the oppressed and the oppressor are involved.[47]

In what has been previously explained regarding the VDMF charism and mission, one can clearly see that the VDMF mission is a question of process and totally depends on the freedom and measure of the participation of the person. Therefore, the experience and learning outcome depend on the active participation of the person in their own faith journey. The VDMF mission does not intend to safeguard a process of knowledge but to spark a process of personal and social transformation that Christian faith offer us. The force of the VDMF mission is that it is dialogical process oriented where God, the person, and the faith community are the main agents. Without dialogue, the process and participation would not take place.

Bevans's and Freire's Contributions

How does Bevans's and Freire's work support participation in the ongoing process of the unfolding of revelation, which is at the core of the VDMF charism and mission? The following will present Bevans's and Freire's contributions to the VDMF mission. The intention is not to apply Bevans's and Freire's concepts to the VDMF mission or to show their effectiveness for divine revelation. Rather, their work will demonstrate the effectiveness of the concepts of prophetic dialogue and *conscientização* in the VDMF mission praxis.

"The response to revelation is not simply a matter of intellectually accepting its content, but, as we read in the constitution *Dei Verbum*, is an attitude in which [a person] 'freely commits [one's] entire self to God.'"[48] Since the Word of God is, in its essence, both personal and relational, it calls for a subjective response in the form of faith on the part of the hearer and receiver of the Word.[49] "The receiving subject is always also part of the concept of 'revelation.' Where there is no one to perceive 'revelation,' no revelation has occurred, because no veil has been removed. By definition,

---

47. VDMF members not only work with the immigrant population but with all cultures and socioeconomic backgrounds. As part of the VDMF ministry, VDMF intentionally organizes multicultural activities where Latinos, Asians, European descent, and Anglo-Saxons, for example, all share and mingle. We bring the oppressed and the oppressor together so that they can learn from each other and change any predisposed cultural preconceived notions, biases, or prejudices. The intention is to have a taste of the reign of God.

48. Wojtyła, *Sources of Renewal*, 53–54.

49. Gourlay, "Understanding of Revelation," 1–10.

Toward a New, Praxis-Oriented Missiology

revelation requires someone who apprehends it."[50] This relational response is essential for revelation.

It was mentioned in chapter 3 that prophetic dialogue contains a pedagogical approach of how to do mission. It is in the pedagogical implications of participation in the ongoing process of revelation where the VDMF mission praxis, Bevans, and Freire intersect and where their work can enrich the VDMF mission. As seen in chapters 1 and 2, one of the riches in Bevans's and Freire's thought is that they do not stay in the cognitive dimension. Also, the transmission of faith is not something static but dynamic, alive, actual, and with a vision toward the future. By using Bevans's and Freire's thought and the VDMF charism, one of the intentions of this entire research is to show that mission is not a question of transmitting knowledge but offering an experiential knowledge of faith. The relational apprehension of revelation is what could make us capable of an experiential assimilation of the good news of the reign of God. Pope Francis, in his encyclical *Lumen Fidei*, states, "Faith is born of an encounter with the living God, who calls us, and reveals his love, a love which precedes us, and upon which we can lean for security, and for building our lives."[51] Therefore, Bevans's notion of mission and Freire's pedagogy very well support and rescue the experiential side of faith and mission, as the Dynamism of the Word in VDMF understanding and practice does.

Additionally, we saw how *conscientização* leads us to understand and undergo a process of awareness within one's own particular reality and context. Simultaneously, prophetic dialogue invites us to a deep listening to the context and the gospel. The Dynamism of the Word starts with the listening of the Word of God. A key element in the transmission of faith is to not depart from an ideal reality. It is this constant listening to the gospel, reality, and context that makes faith dynamic and not be put into a box or a structure but alive and always new.

Bevans and Freire highlight the importance of the mutual learning process from the one performing the action (doing mission, accompanying, or teaching) and the one receiving it. The vulnerability and humility of acknowledging that we can always learn from each other and that we are unfinished contains an inherent wisdom that leaves room for an experiential practice. The VDMF way of praying and teaching how to pray with the Word of God illustrates of this point. If one approaches scripture believing

---

50. Ratzinger, *Milestones*, 108–9.
51. *Lumen Fidei*, no. 4.

that one knows everything and there is nothing new to pray, to discover, to be open to, then there is no room for a new experience of God and of faith. In the same way, if I perform my ministry with Latino immigrant people thinking that I know everything, then the process of the Wheel of Metanoia would not take place and would not spin.

One of the riches of prophetic dialogue is that it offers an approach to mission with profound openness, presence, and respect for the other. Similarly, the process of *conscientização* allows one not only to encounter the other where they are but also respects the uniqueness of every person, culture, church, and society. This profound and respectful approach is essential for the VDMF mission; but it can be easily lost. The reason is because the core of the VDMF charism is the personal and loving friendship with God. Since this is such a personal and unique experience, there is the constant danger of making one's own experience of God absolute. Being enclosed in this shadow places the person on the opposite side of humility. Consequently, there is no openness, presence, or respect for the uniqueness of the person and culture (even to God). Therefore, the process of revelation or the Wheel of Metanoia stops.

We also have seen the importance of dialogue in mission. Dialogue is an essential tool to help the person become a subject and not an object, and as Bevans says, it helps one to approach mission with bare feet and *do it in vulnerability and in humility*. Without dialogue, there is no participation in the process of revelation and fellowship. Moreover, without dialogue, there is no contextualization of the gospel, there is no process of *conscientização*, and announcing and incarnating the gospel will become imposing. This chapter showed in the understanding of the VDMF charism how incarnation is based on a dialogical process.

In summary, the contributions of prophetic dialogue and *conscientização* to mission praxis, in light of the VDMF mission, are the following: (1) a process of active participation that makes transmission of faith experiential, (2) a mission approach marked by a mutual learning process, (3) social transformation that is mutual (oppressed and oppressor), and (4) a relational response to divine revelation. As mentioned previously, the response to revelation is not simply a matter of intellectually accepting its content; rather, it is an attitude in which a person freely commits oneself to God.

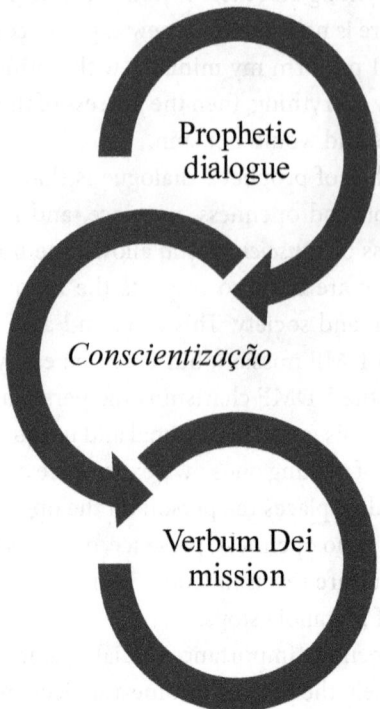

Figure 4.2. Prophetic dialogue, *conscientização*, and Verbum Dei charism connecting.

CONCLUDING THOUGHTS

Indubitably, prophetic dialogue, *conscientização*, and the VDMF mission aim at social transformation. On this point, "The Herald of the Evangelizer," a document written by Bonet Bonet for the VDMF community, provides insight. "The Herald of the Evangelizer" is a heartfelt manifesto and guiding tool for evangelization.[52] This text offers a parallel work that

---

52. "The Herald of the Evangelizer" is a manifesto in poetic form by Bonet Bonet. It was written in Medellín, Colombia, in 1979, as a consequence of his vision for the world. At that time, Colombia's political situation was precarious. He was directing spiritual exercises for members of the VDMF when he wrote "The Herald of the Evangelizer." The text expresses Bonet Bonet's heart and his dream for this world. It is a reflection on concrete situations and sufferings of the people and calls for an authentic living of the good news. It contains three major parts: (1) why do I want to evangelize? (written in May 1979), (2) the mission of the evangelizer (written in June 7, 1979), and (3) the evangelizer (written in June 15, 1979).

Contribution to the Praxis and Field of Missiology

deeply resonates with Bevans's and Freire's social transformation approach. It expresses the desire, need, and urgency for evangelization:

> Why do I want to evangelize, to announce the Good News of the Kingdom? Why do I want to dedicate myself to the propagation of the Faith to the ends of the earth? Why do I want to preach the Gospel of Jesus of Nazareth and consecrate the whole of my life to prayer and ministry of the Word? Why evangelize, and for what?[53]

There are two important aspects in social transformation presented by Bonet Bonet that are related to Bevans's and Freire's thought. First, Bonet Bonet envisioned a freedom and liberation based on the good news and the anticipation of the reign of God. This embodies the prophetic element that we saw in chapter 1 regarding prophetic dialogue: the one who announces and denounces the social structures of injustice and are committed to a radical process of transforming the world act in a prophetic manner. Similarly, one of the intended objectives of *conscientização* is to denounce dehumanizing structures and to announce a structure that will humanize. "The Herald of the Evangelizer" shows how Bonet Bonet denounces unjust structures by addressing different sources of poverty and suffering that afflicts humankind:

> Because I want to put into movement so many paralyzed lives that are without direction or meaning, without the desire to live; lives that are bored and lethargic, with doubts and suspicions, uncertainty and indecision; lives that are empty and broken by disabling complexes.
>
> Because I long for families to enjoy the warmth of a loving home, instead of the cold atmosphere of a cemetery, without even the embers of love and intimacy, affection and care, and the spontaneity and joy that is fruitful and creative.[54]

In other words, social transformation entails denouncing unjust structures, which is a clearly defined process in prophetic dialogue, *conscientização*, and the VDMF charism.

Second, for Bonet Bonet, the proclamation of the good news of the reign of God is essential to the process of liberation of the world, which is a process that is personal but also communal. Thus, liberation is the consequence or purpose of social transformation. Bonet Bonet's manifesto is a

---

53. Bonet Bonet, "Herald of the Evangelizer," 1.
54. Bonet Bonet, "Herald of the Evangelizer," 1.

Toward a New, Praxis-Oriented Missiology

clear call to all nations to stop war and to see beauty in all living creatures, especially in all God's children:

> I am interested and fascinated to announce the Good News of the Kingdom; a Kingdom of peace and justice; a Kingdom of Life and Love, in order to stop the relentless war between different countries and races, of one continent against the other, between nations and races, detaining the fratricidal struggle between brothers and sisters, and of children against parents.[55]

Bonet Bonet envisioned the liberation of men and women of today through the proclamation of the gospel and the notion of the kingdom of justice, love, and peace. We also have seen that the process of prophetic dialogue and *conscientização* intends a social transformation that leads to liberation. In other words, there is no social transformation without liberation and vice versa.

Lastly, prophetic dialogue, *conscientização*, and the VDMF charism have nothing to do with mastering techniques to guarantee a "successful" mission approach. They promote, rather, a process of active participation in God's self-revelation. They remind us, again, to remain open, alert, and attentive in our encounter with the world and the other in it, all the while continuously incarnating the good news of the reign of God.

This chapter explored some of the missiological implications regarding the praxis approach in the VDMF mission when using the concepts of prophetic dialogue and *conscientização*. It introduced the Verbum Dei charism and mission and showed how the concepts of prophetic dialogue and *conscientização* are effective to VDMF mission praxis: a relational response to divine revelation, a transmission of faith that is experiential, a mission approach with a mutual learning process from the one doing the mission work and the one receiving it, and a social transformation that is a mutual process (oppressed and oppressor).

---

55. Bonet Bonet, "Herald of the Evangelizer," 1.

Conclusion

Eu também alentados por testemunhos de gratuita amorosidade à vida, que fortalecem, em nós, a necessária, mas às vezes combalida esperança.[1]

—PAULO FREIRE, *PEDAGOGY OF INDIGNATION*

As I LOOK BACK at this work and to the way I tried to engage my ministry, I found a lot of resonance in Freire's words: *There is no possibility of thinking of tomorrow without being encouraged by testimonies of gratuitous loving of life*, which have strengthened in us a much needed hope. What carried me through this research process was to perceive the authenticity and testimony of the life of Bonet Bonet, of the life of Freire, and of the work of Bevans when rescuing the transformative and liberating process that the VDMF mission praxis and the concepts of prophetic dialogue and *conscientização* entail. At the end of this work, I feel a sense of hope toward the future of the mission of the church because, undoubtedly, prophetic dialogue, *conscientização*, and the VDMF charism could thoroughly enrich and offer a new lens to twenty-first-century mission praxis. The following will present some of the major findings and overall relevance of this work.

A new self-understanding of the church emerged after the Second Vatican Council, which greatly affected the theology of mission. Mission

---

1. "There is no possibility of thinking of tomorrow without being encouraged by testimonies of gratuitous loving of life, which strengthen in us that so-needed and at times embattled hope." Freire, *Pedagogy of Indignation*, 103.

Toward a New, Praxis-Oriented Missiology

is no longer conceived as an activity of the church but as the movement of God to and in the world. The church is a simple instrument to continue collaborating in the *missio Dei*. Additionally, there is new awareness that mission requires a conscious dedication, preparation, and commitment to incarnate the gospel in every culture. Mission is not just a matter of doing things for people. Thus, to support the process of incarnating the gospel, there must be dialogue, respect, constant listening, an openness to the signs of the times, a willingness to learn, and a sense of contemplation so that one could perceive a particular context in a new way and recognize the presence of God in every culture.

The concept of mission as prophetic dialogue intends to capture the truth of the three main strains that characterized mission theology in the late twentieth century from a Roman Catholic perspective: (1) mission as participation in the life and mission of the Trinitarian God, (2) mission as establishing the reign of God within all creation, and (3) mission as emphasizing the centrality of Christ and the importance of sharing God's truth with humankind. The proposed synthesis of these three strains is mission as prophetic dialogue, which provides a more adequate model of mission for the twenty-first century.

One can conclude that the praxis of mission as prophetic dialogue is not something new and unique in Bevans's work and thought. The church's documents after the Second Vatican Council disclosed the need to do mission in dialogue and at the same time stressed the importance of the prophetic element of the gospel. The church is more aware that she has to become what she proclaims. Therefore, dialogue and prophecy cannot be separated. However, the call to be more intentional in doing mission with a prophetic dialogue hermeneutic is novel in Bevans's work, and his understanding of contextual theology as prophetic dialogue is unique. Bevans is not limiting theology to pure reflexive thinking (as it was done in the past). For him, prophetic dialogue and contextual theology reflect the mission of God. The Word has the full capacity of being incarnated in all human contexts. Therefore, theology and mission should be done in a dialectic openness, acknowledging the present human experience of every culture and context, with fidelity to scripture and tradition. For Bevans, theology and mission cannot be separated. Prophetic dialogue as contextual theology offers a constant reflection, a constructive critique, and a more applicable theology and mission in the concrete realities of peoples and times. Using prophetic dialogue as a hermeneutic to do theology and mission offers us a

Conclusion

constant reflection of how the understanding and praxis of faith is continuously shaped by the culture and context. Therefore, prophetic dialogue is not a successful method to do mission but a constant listening and adaptation to the different contexts and to the signs of the times.

Also, Bevans's proposal is a praxis of mission in dialogical prophecy. When approaching a mission/ministerial setting, the question to ponder is not, is it dialogue or prophecy that needs to be applied? Rather, the question is, when can a dialogical setting be employed and when can one act prophetically? For this discernment, it is important to be open, to listen, and to recognize the presence of God in every culture and context. Prophetic dialogue is not just one more missiological approach to understanding the reasons for doing mission. Rather, prophetic dialogue contains a clear pedagogical approach of "how" to do mission. This approach is deepened when combined with Freire's concept of *conscientização*.

When introducing Freire's work in chapter 2, there was an intentional emphasis on Freire's life experience and limit-situations in order to rescue Freire's legacy and spirit. The intention was not to simply present Freire's method with its concrete steps and stages that "successfully" leads to a *conscientização* process in the person. Freire was completely against importing and exporting his ideas. He did not want his pedagogical proposal to get stuck into a technique or be an interesting concept to look at. Therefore, in order to find *conscientização* applicable to our present time, it is important to situate the concept within Freire's life experience and struggles in his personal, work, and academic life and in his specific Third World economic and sociopolitical context. For Freire, the process of *conscientização* is individual and collective and involves action and reflection. As mentioned in chapter 2, *conscientização* is based upon a dialectical and phenomenological approach to how consciousness and the world interact. It calls human beings to act consciously on concrete reality. Though *conscientização* is reflective and practice based, it is not sufficient or an end in itself. *Conscientização* without dialogue cannot in and of itself lead to any kind of transformation. Dialogue is necessary to unfold a process of *conscientização*, hence the need to relate Freire's *conscientização* with Bevans's prophetic dialogue.

Chapter 3 showed how Freire's work on *conscientização* can enrich Bevan's work on prophetic dialogue and vice versa. The aim of both concepts is not to offer or seek a specific method or technique or even to produce a specific result. Rather, both concepts attempt to rescue a process that is inherently dialogical, reciprocal, transformative, and liberating. By rescuing

Toward a New, Praxis-Oriented Missiology

this process, one can grasp the relevance of the pedagogical implications of *conscientização* and prophetic dialogue. These implications include but are not limited to the following: the gospel can be incarnated in every culture, mission praxis can be more critically and theologically appropriate, and the transmission of faith is more experiential and not simply doctrinal.

In order to display an overall relevance of Bevans's and Freire's thought, chapter 4 turned toward their pedagogical implications present in the VDMF mission praxis and charism, which follow the ongoing process of divine revelation.[2] First, we have seen that the aim of prophetic dialogue or *conscientização* is not cognitive knowledge. Second, we saw in chapter 3 that transmission of faith is not something static but dynamic, alive, actual, and with a vision toward the future. Moreover, the response to revelation is not a matter of intellectually accepting its content. The apprehension of revelation is relational and impacts the whole being of a person because it is about a personal encounter with Jesus Christ. Third, the subject matter of faith has the potential to give an answer to human questions and problems of believers from all ages (past, present, and future) and equip believers with the capacity to live with more questions. One of the intentions of this entire research is to show that mission endeavor is not just a question of transmitting knowledge. Handing on the faith, or proclaiming the good news of the reign of God, must be alive and must be experienced in practice. People pursue the experience that faith offers something relevant for one's own life. Thus, it is important to offer an experiential knowledge of faith. Lastly, this experiential aspect of the transmission of faith is the principal connecting point between Bevans, Freire, and the VDMF charism and mission. To lead the person to a process of knowing one's faith in an experiential way has specific pedagogical implications. Therefore, prophetic dialogue offers an awareness of meeting people where they are, with openness to their traditions, culture, and experience, recognizing the validity of people's own religious existence and integrity of their own religious ends. Freire's process of *conscientização* significantly supports this experiential and relational apprehension of faith/divine revelation. And the VDMF mission guides the person to an experiential knowledge of God and of the Christian faith that leads one to a profound personal transformation and a deep social commitment.

Chapter 4 also talked about how people who pray with the Word of God enter a liberation and transformative process, as seen in the Wheel

2. *Dei Verbum*, no. 2.

Conclusion

of Metanoia. The process of *conscientização* in combination with the Dynamism of the Word (it is important to remember that the Dynamism of the Word is not a prayer practice but a way of life, a process of individual and social transformation originated through the steps of listening, assimilating, living, and giving the Word) make it possible for people to insert themselves critically into their historical reality while transforming it. In other words, *conscientização* with the Dynamism of the Word include the combination of one's own reflection on the world and one's own action on it. Liberation is not given simply by desiring it or by self-accomplishment. It is a slow process that requires the participation of the person and the grace of God. We saw in my ministry with the Latino immigrant population how Freire's process of *conscientização* supports the dynamism of VDMF mission.[3]

With regard to the VDMF mission, there is so much richness that the VDMF charism can offer to our twenty-first-century church and world. Like Bevans's and Freire's proposal, the VDMF charism is based on process, and the unfolding of it relies on the freedom and measure of the participation of the person. As we have seen, the experience of faith and the learning outcome require the active participation of the person in one's own faith journey. The VDMF mission, as prophetic dialogue and *conscientização*, does not intend to guarantee faith knowledge (though doctrinal elements are always imparted) but to lead the person to a process of personal and social transformation. One can agree that the force of VDMF mission, prophetic dialogue,

---

3. As a side note, because of allusions to Freire's work, I make reference to Rev. Pedro Arrupe, SJ (1907–1991), the 28th Superior General of the Society of Jesus. He led the Jesuits in serving church and society in a post-Second Vatican Council world and was a man of great spiritual depth and with a deep commitment to social justice. In Arrupe's talk about Decree 4 of the 32nd General Congregation of the Society of Jesus, where he elaborates on practical aspects of faith and justice, he uses the concept of *conscientização* and refers to Freire's work. Arrupe expresses that for an "inner disposition of spirit, so necessary for a real discernment, we also need as complete and deep a knowledge as possible of the reality that is the object of our discernment, so that we can discover in that reality the expression of God's will for the world. To discover that, we need, first of all, a real 'conscientization,' or critical contact with reality." Arrupe, "Some Far-Reaching Vistas," 147. Arrupe clearly states that conscientization is not merely to contemplate reality (this is false intellectualism): "There can be no conscientization apart from practical action. The dialectical unity 'action-reflection' will always be [one's] . . . only effective way of changing the world." Arrupe, "Some Far-Reaching Vistas," 148. I am taken by the resonances between Arrupe's way of promoting social transformation and commitment and that of Bevans's, Freire's, and the VDMF's core insights described in this research.

Toward a New, Praxis-Oriented Missiology

and *conscientização* is a dialogical process orientation where God's grace, the person, and the community are the main agents.

At the end of this research, I can say that "the" successful missionary method does not exist and cannot exist. What Bevans, Freire, and the VDMF charism can teach us is that "the wheel turns full circle again" because faith is dynamic, alive, actual, and fore-sighting the future. The hope is that we had acquired some tools to not make one's own experience of God, of faith, or of mission absolute but to have the humility to constantly be open and present to read reality with new awareness, respecting the uniqueness of the person and culture and knowing that our interaction with the world remakes it.

Though not affecting the substance within the scope of this research, there are limitations to Bevans's prophetic dialogue and Freire's *conscientização* that should be considered when further research is done in this area. In the following, I share some of those limitations.

Although prophetic dialogue contains a pedagogical approach, one needs to take into account colonialist structures when approaching realities of internalized oppression when working with cultures that have been oppressed for a long time. We cannot be naïve about the mechanisms and social structures of oppression that have become interwoven in the very fabric of such cultures, which then manifest in the people themselves. One of the remaining questions regarding the practice of the concept of mission as prophetic dialogue is, how much does it take into account the complexity of the consequences of colonialization? It is not clear how Bevans's concept of prophetic dialogue takes these complex social and personal underlying structures into consideration. Sometimes colonialized configurations are so profound and so perpetuated that one should question if prophetic dialogue can unfold in those settings. In other words, to what extent can the oppressive structures influence and even paralyze a mission approach as prophetic dialogue?[4]

---

4. For example, how can prophetic dialogue be applied to subaltern women? I would like to make reference to Gayatri Chakravorty Spivak's article, "Can the Subaltern Speak?" Using a postcolonial lens, she focuses on female subaltern from the Third World. These women became the silenced burden of Western imperialism. For Spivak, speech provides spaces of power and access; however, subaltern women do not have access to speech. She says that the subaltern cannot speak because they have been silenced for so long. Based on Spivak's research, Ania Loomba arrives at the conclusion that colonial powers managed to silence the colonized to the extent that the colonized become victims or romanticize the image of the colonized. Thus, they overlook the oppression they experience. How to overcome the oppressive structures through prophetic dialogue when

Conclusion

Regarding Freire, it is important to mention that he was constantly criticized for being an idealist or dreamer because he believed that social transformation could be possible through a process of *conscientização*. Many praised and valued Freire's work, but also many (on the right and also on the left) do not agree or see a positive influence in his contributions. In the initial state of this research when deciding to use Freire's work, I had a very enthusiastic and positive view of Freire's revolutionary pedagogical contributions because that was my experience as a student of pedagogy. Subsequently, when fulfilling the course work of my doctoral studies, I took a class at the University of California, Berkeley, on critical pedagogy with a focus on Freire's work (he is considered the father of critical pedagogy). There, my eyes were opened to the many criticisms to his work from a critical theory point of view. When learning about the potential dangers of his thought, I was losing hope and questioning Freire's legacy. Some of the major criticisms to his work include (1) Freire as the oppressor who developed a pedagogy for the oppressed, (2) Freire's ideologization of the oppressed can be easily dismissed for comfortable utopianism, otherworldly mysticism, and irrelevance, (3) the use of Freire's pedagogical method with the assumption that his liberating educational processes will be transformative, (4) the abstract and sometimes mystical nature of his writings which do not directly address the specificity of oppression, internal contradiction of political projects, or the ambiguities of history.[5] All these and many more criticisms left me rest-

---

approaching realities like this one? Spivak, "Can the Subaltern Speak?," 21–80. See also Loomba, *Colonialism/Postcolonialism*.

5. For more information on Freire's critics, see Weiler, "Myths of Paulo Freire," 353–71; Lankshear and McLaren, *Politics of Liberation*. Also, in the Brazilian senate, a bill was introduced in September 2017 to revoke the law that made Freire the Patron of Brazilian Education. What the senate questions is the collapse of Brazilian education, the loss of intellectual life, and forms of ideological influence of children on the ideology of gender choice into the curriculum and normalization of certain types of art that for some is perceived morally offensive. The speculation is that all these ideologies have been constructed as the logical consequence of Freirean pedagogy. The issue is described as raising consciousness under the semblance of freedom of expression at the expense of degrading basic international standards of education, weakening social decency, undermining moral values within families, and devitalizing good citizenship (corruption that is praised rather than consigned). Those could probably be strong affirmations of some consequences of Freire's pedagogy, but what I would like to highlight in here is the possible conceptions of Freire's pedagogical ideas. To follow the news about the Brazilian senate bill, one can consult the following: "Instituto Repudia Revogação de Título de Patrono da Educação de Paulo Freire," Brasil 247, last modified June 26, 2018, https://www.brasil247.com/cultura/instituto-repudia-revogacao-de-titulo-de-patrono-da-educacao-de-paulo-freire; "Sugestão Popular Quer Retirar de Paulo Freire o Título

Toward a New, Praxis-Oriented Missiology

less and with the deep question of whether Freire's work could continue to be valid for the twenty-first century. I therefore threw myself into the study of Freire's spirit and motivation to develop his pedagogy, especially since my experience and judgment still convinced me that *conscientização* is an authentic process important to uphold.

In this final thought, I would like to provide a glimpse of a future perspective for developing the importance of understanding the church's mission for a better understanding of the church herself. For this, I will use some of the most recent ideas regarding mission found in Andrew Walls, Bevans, and Schroeder.

Walls talks about "mission from anywhere to anywhere."[6] He points out that the church has no single center but many centers. There has been a period of Christian history when it seemed that Christianity belonged to the West. However, the global character of Christianity is obvious. Walls argues that the "Church and mission are multi-centric, but the different centers belong to a single organism. Christian faith is embodied faith; Christ takes flesh again among those who respond to him in faith. But there is no generalized humanity; incarnation has always to be culture-specific."[7] Two aspects from Walls's proposal are worth highlighting: (1) The global character of Christianity reveals the need for an understanding of the church and mission as multi-centric. One could agree that mission as prophetic dialogue provides an adequate model of mission for a multi-centric church. (2) Incarnation always has to be culture specific. We saw how VDMF spirituality is focused on increased participation in the ongoing process of the unfolding of divine revelation in this world (a concept reflected in the Second Vatican Council document *Dei Verbum*). With this understanding, mission shifts to a participation in the process of incarnating the Word in specific cultures. These aspects from Wall's proposal are essential for understanding the church's mission and of herself.

Additionally, it was mentioned in the beginning of this section that the new understanding of mission goes hand in hand with the new self-understanding of the church. To further develop a theology of mission that encompasses the global, multi-centric, and ecumenical reality of the church

---

de Patrono da Educação Brasileira," Senado Noticias, last modified November 24, 2017, https://www12.senado.leg.br/noticias/audios/2017/11/sugestao-popular-quer-revogar-de-paulo-freire-o-titulo-de-patrono-da-educacao-brasileira.

6. Walls, "Christian Mission," 202.

7. Walls, "Christian Mission," 203.

Conclusion

in today's postmodern and postcolonial world, the church needs to recognize the priority of her mission for an understanding of herself. In their article "Missionary Ecclesiology: Evangelical, Ecumenical, and Catholic Developments in 'Engaging the Nations,'" Bevans and Schroeder present the importance of a "missionary ecclesiology."[8] They say that this missionary ecclesiology has been a minority voice.[9] However, in the Roman Catholic tradition, the new missionary ecclesiology is slowly emerging. The Second Vatican Council's Decree on the Mission Activity of the Church emphasizes this missionary perspective: "The pilgrim church is missionary by its very nature."[10] This missionary ecclesiology is important because "we believe that a church that recognizes its essential missionary nature, and organizes itself accordingly, is the most adequate way to do ecclesiology today."[11] One could say that ecclesiology is missionary in the sense that mission is understood incarnationally and relationally, which is essential to the church's self-understanding. One could see the *missio Dei* as the contextual and missionary "located-ness" of the Christian community and the dynamic of the gospel engaging with human cultures. Their convergence provides a foundation for the continuing development of a missional ecclesiology.

With the hope that this work could contribute toward "missionary methods" (an area of missiology that some would say has hardly been developed) and to continue supporting the importance of mission as the identity of the church, I would like to end with some words from Freire's last book *Pedagogy of Freedom*, which expresses the relevance of our presence in this world and the transcendence of what we can construct in it.

> I like being human because I perceive that the construction of my presence in the world, which is a construction involving others and is subject to generic factors, is nonetheless a presence whose construction has much to do with myself. It will be ironic if the awareness of my presence in the world did not at the same time

---

8. Protestant and Evangelical circles use the term "missional ecclesiology." "The term missional was coined to reflect the understanding that mission is not simply a sub-category of ecclesiology, but belongs to the essence of what it means to be the Church. The Church does not 'do' mission; rather, the Church 'is' mission. The Church does not 'have' a mission; God has created a sent-Church, a missional Church. This view is based on the missional or sending nature of God as God sends his Son, his Spirit, and his Church into the world." Franklin, "Bonhoeffer's Missional Ecclesiology," 97.

9. Bevans and Schroeder, "Missionary Ecclesiology," 57–67.

10. *Ad Gentes*, no. 2.

11. Bevans and Schroeder, "Missionary Ecclesiology," 67.

Toward a New, Praxis-Oriented Missiology

imply recognition that I could not be absent from the construction of my own presence.... I like being a human person because even though I know that the material, social, political, cultural, and ideological conditions in which we find ourselves almost always generate divisions that make difficult the construction of our ideals of change and transformation, I know also that the obstacles are not eternal.[12]

---

12. Freire, *Pedagogy of Freedom*, 54–55.

Bibliography

Allen, Roland. *Missionary Methods: God's Plan for Missions according to Paul*. Abbotsford, WI: Aneko, 2017.

———. *Missionary Methods: St. Paul's or Ours*. Grand Rapids: Eerdmans, 1964.

Amalados, Michael. "Mission as Prophecy." In Scherer and Bevans, *Theological Foundations*, 64–72.

Antes, Peter, and Hans Waldenfels. "Mission in Non-Christian Religions." In Müller et al., *Dictionary of Mission*, 303–7.

Araújo Freire, Ana Maria. "Paulo Freire: Sua Vida, Sua Obra." *Educação em Revista* 2 (2001) 1–13. http://www2.marilia.unesp.br/ revistas/index.php/educacaoemrevista/article/view/663/546.

Araújo Freire, Ana Maria, and Donaldo Macedo, eds. *The Paulo Freire Reader*. New York: Continuum, 1998.

Arrupe, Pedro. "Some Far-Reaching Vistas of Decree 4 of GC 32." In *Justice with Faith Today*, edited by Jerome Aixala, 2:141–70. St. Louis: Institute of Jesuit Sources, 1980.

Azevedo, Marcello de C. "Basic Ecclesial Communities." In *Mysterium Liberationis: Fundamental Concepts of Liberation Theology*, edited by Ignacio Ellacuría and Jon Sobrino, 636–53. Maryknoll: Orbis, 1993.

Barrett, David B., et al., eds. *World Christian Encyclopedia: A Comparative Survey of Churches and Religions in the Modern World*. Vol. 1, *The World by Countries: Religionists, Churches, Ministries*. 2nd ed. Oxford: Oxford University Press, 2001.

Barroso Tristan, Jose Maria. "Giroux: The Necessity of Critical Pedagogy in Dark Times." *Global Education Magazine*, February 6, 2013. http://www.truth-out.org/news/item/14331-a-critical-interview-with-henry-giroux.

Beaver, Robert Pierce. "The Legacy of Rufus Anderson." *Occasional Bulletin of Missionary Research* 3 (1979) 94–97.

Bevans, Stephen B. "Contextual Theology and Prophetic Dialogue." In *Mission on the Road to Emmaus*, edited by Cathy Ross and Stephen B. Bevans, 227–37. Maryknoll: Orbis, 2015.

Bibliography

———. "Interfaith Engagement as Prophetic Dialogue." *Evangelical Interfaith Dialogue* (Fall 2014) 13–15. https://fullerstudio.fuller.edu/wp-content/uploads/2017/03/EIFD_2014_Fall.pdf.

———. "Migration and Mission: Pastoral Challenges, Theological Insights." In *Contemporary Issues of Migration and Theology*, edited by Elaine Padilla and Peter C. Phan, 157–78. New York: Palgrave Macmillan, 2013.

———. "Missiology through the Back Door: Reflections of an SVD Mission Theologian." *Verbum SVD* 52 (2011) 367–77.

———. "Models of Contextual Theology." *Missiology: An International Review* 13 (1985) 185–202.

———. *Models of Contextual Theology*. Rev. ed. Maryknoll: Orbis, 2011.

———. "A Prophetic Dialogue Approach." In *The Mission of the Church: Five Views in Conversation*, edited by Craig Otto, 3–20. Grand Rapids: Baker Academic, 2016.

———. "Seeing Mission through Images." In Scherer and Bevans, *Theological Foundations*, 158–69.

———. "A Theology of Mission for the Church of the Twenty-First Century: Mission as Prophetic Dialogue." In Bevans and Tahaafe-Williams, *Contextual Theology for the Twenty-First Century*, 99–108.

———. "What Has Contextual Theology to Offer the Church of the Twenty-First Century?" In Bevans and Tahaafe-Williams, *Contextual Theology for the Twenty-First Century*, 3–17.

Bevans, Stephen, and Jeffrey Gros. *Evangelization and Religious Freedom: Ad Gentes, Dignitatis Humanae*. New York: Paulist, 2009.

Bevans, Stephen B., and Roger P. Schroeder. *Constants in Context: A Theology of Mission for Today*. Maryknoll: Orbis, 2004.

———. "Missionary Ecclesiology: Evangelical, Ecumenical, and Catholic Developments in 'Engaging the Nations.'" In *Contemporary Mission Theology: Engaging the Nations*, edited by Robert L. Gallagher and Paul Hertig, 57–67. New York: Orbis, 2017.

———. *Prophetic Dialogue: Reflections on Christian Mission Today*. Maryknoll: Orbis, 2011.

———. "'We Were Gentle Among You': Christian Mission as Dialogue." *Australian eJournal of Theology* 7 (2006) 1–17. http://aejt.com.au/__data/assets/pdf_file/0011/395129/AEJT_7.3_Bevans_Schroeder_Gentle_Among_You.pdf.

Bevans, Stephen B., and Katalina Tahaafe-Williams, eds. *Contextual Theology for the Twenty-First Century*. Eugene, OR: Pickwick, 2011.

Bonet Bonet, Jaime. "Breve Ideario." 1969. Generalate of the VDMF, Rome.

———. *Familiares de Dios*. Siete Aguas, Valencia: Fundación Barceló, 1999.

———. "The Herald of the Evangelizer." 1969. Generalate of the VDMF, Rome.

———. "Statutes of the Verbum Dei Missionary Fraternity." 2nd ed. 1993. Generalate of the VDMF, Rome.

Bitter, Gottfried. "What Faith Shall We Hand On? Can It Be Reduced to Kerygmatic Essentials?" In Greinacher and Elizondo, *Transmission of Christian Faith*, 39–44.

Boff, Leonardo. *Trinity and Society*. Eugene, OR: Wipf & Stock, 1988.

Boff, Leonardo, and Clodovis Boff. *Introducing Liberation Theology*. Maryknoll: Orbis, 1987.

Bosch, David J. *Transforming Mission: Paradigm Shifts in Mission Theology*. 20th anniversary ed. Maryknoll: Orbis, 2011.

Bibliography

Callahan, William. "The Evangelization of Franco's 'New Spain.'" *Church History* 56 D (1987) 491–503.
Christian, Robert G. "The Enduring Wisdom of Emmanuel Mounier." *Church Life* 3 (2015) 12–14. http://liturgy.nd.edu/assets/172339/christian_enduringwisdomofemmanuel mounier_vol3issue4.pdf.
Collins, Denis. *Paulo Freire: His Life, Works and Thoughts*. New York: Paulist, 1977.
———. *Paulo Freire: Una Filosofía Educativa para Nuestro Tiempo*. Mexico City: Universidad La Salle, 2000.
———. "Two Utopians: A Comparison and Contrast of the Educational Philosophies of Paulo Freire and Theodore Brameld." Ed.D. diss., University of Southern California, 1973.
Congar, Yves. *I Believe in the Holy Spirit*. Translated by David Smith. New York: Seabury, 1983.
———. *Lay People in the Church: A Study for a Theology of Laity*. 2nd ed. Translated by Donald Attwater. Westminster, MD: Newman, 1965.
———. *True and False Reform in the Church*. Translated by Paul Philibert. Collegeville: Liturgical, 2011.
Constitutions of the Verbum Dei Missionary Fraternity. February 6, 2012. Generalate of the VDMF, Rome.
Costas, Orlando E. *Christ Outside the Gate: Mission beyond Christendom*. Maryknoll: Orbis, 1982.
Dale, John, and Emery J. Hyslop-Margison. *Paulo Freire: Teaching for Freedom and Transformation; The Philosophical Influences on the Work of Paulo Freire*. New York: Springer, 2010.
D'Ambrosio, Marcellino. "Ressourcement Theology, Aggiornamento, and the Hermeneutics of Tradition." *Communio* 18 (1991) 530–55.
Decreto of the Congregazione per gli Istituti di Vita Consatrata e le Societá di Vita Apostolica. Prot. n. MA. 2-1/98. April 15, 2000. Vatican City State.
Decreto of the Congregazione per gli Istituti di Vita Consatrata e le Societá di Vita Apostolica. Prot. n. MA. 2-1/98. February 27, 2012. Vatican City State.
Donohue, John W. "Paulo Freire: Philosopher of Adult Education." *America*, September 16, 1972.
Donovan, Vincent. *Christianity Rediscovered*. 25th anniversary ed. Maryknoll: Orbis, 2003.
Dorr, Donal. *Mission in Today's World*. Maryknoll: Orbis, 2000.
Duarte, Eduardo Manuel. "Thinking Together as One: Freire's Rewriting of Husserl." In *Philosophy of Education 2000*, edited by Lynda Stone, 180–88. Chapel Hill: University of North Carolina, 2000. https://pdfs.semanticscholar.org/e8c7/b29b0181e6edf3b4fac85eb303cc4eec19b6.pdf.
Dulles, Avery. *The Catholicity of the Church*. New York: Oxford, 1989.
Emmott, D. H. "Alexander Duff and the Foundation of Modern Education in India." *British Journal of Education Studies* 13 (1965) 160–69.
Ezquerda Bifet, Juan. *Diccionario de la Evangelización*. Madrid: Editorial BAC, 1998.
———. *Misionología: Evangelizar en un Mundo Global*. Madrid: Editorial BAC, 2008.
Feenberg, Andrew. *The Philosophy of Praxis: Marx, Lukács and the Frankfurt School*. Brooklyn: Verso, 2014.
Fowler, James. "A Gradual Introduction into the Faith." In Greinacher and Elizondo, *Transmission of Christian Faith*, 47–53.

Bibliography

Francis. Address to Members of the Pontifical Commission for Latin America, February 28, 2014. http://w2.vatican.va/content/francesco/en/speeches/2014/february/documents/papa-francesco_20140228_pontificia-commissione-america-latina.html.

———. *Lumen Fidei*. Encyclical on Faith, June 29, 2013. http://w2.vatican.va/content/francesco/en/encyclicals/documents/papa-francesco_20130629_enciclica-lumen-fidei.html.

Franklin, Patrick. "Bonhoeffer's Missional Ecclesiology." *McMaster Journal of Theology and Ministry* 9 (2007–2008) 96–128.

Freire, Paulo. *Cartas a Cristina: Reflexiones Sobre Mi Vida y Mi Trabajo*. Mexico City: Editorial Siglo Veintiuno, 2015.

———. *Cartas a Cristina: Reflexões Sobre Minha Vida e Minha Práxis*. Rio de Janeiro: Edições Paz e Terra, 1994.

———. "Conscientisation." *Cross Currents* 24 (1974) 23–31.

———. *Cultural Action for Freedom*. 2000 ed. Cambridge: Harvard University Press, 2000.

———. *La Educación como Practica de la Libertad*. Quincuagesimocuarta reimpresión. Mexico City: Editorial Siglo Veintiuno, 2011.

———. *Education for Critical Consciousness*. New York: Continuum, 2008.

———. *Education: The Practice of Freedom*. London: Writers and Readers Publishing Cooperative, 1976.

———. "Learning to Question: A Pedagogy of Liberation." In Araújo Freire and Macedo, *Paulo Freire Reader*, 186–230.

———. *Pedagogia da Esperança: Um Reencontro Com a Pedagogia do Oprimido*. Rio de Janeiro: Editora Paz e Terra, 1992.

———. *Pedagogia da Indignação: Cartas Pedagógicas e Outros Escritos*. São Paulo: Editora UNESP, 2000.

———. *Pedagogía de la Autonomía: Saberes Necesarios para la Práctica Educativa*. Mexico City: Editorial Siglo Veintiuno, 1997.

———. *Pedagogia do Oprimido*. Rio de Janeiro: Edições Paz e Terra, 1987.

———. *Pedagogy of Freedom: Ethics, Democracy, and Civic Courage*. New York: Rowman and Littlefield, 1999.

———. *Pedagogy of Hope: Reliving Pedagogy of the Oppressed*. New York: Continuum, 2004.

———. *Pedagogy of Indignation*. Boulder, CO: Paradigm, 2004.

———. *Pedagogy of the Heart*. New York: Continuum, 1998.

———. *Pedagogy of the Oppressed*. 30th anniversary ed. New York: Continuum, 2011.

———. *Teachers as Cultural Workers: Letters to Those Who Dare to Teach*. Cambridge, MA: Westview, 2005.

Freire, Paulo, and Antonio Faundez. *Learning to Question: A Pedagogy of Liberation*. New York: Continuum, 1989.

Freire, Paulo, and Ira Shor. *Medo e Ousadia: O Cotidiano do Professor*. Rio de Janeiro: Edições Paz e Terra, 1986.

Gadotti, Moacir. *Reading Paulo Freire, His Life and Work*. Albany: State University of New York Press, 1994.

Giroux, Henry A. *On Critical Pedagogy*. New York: Continuum, 2011.

Gourlay, Thomas. "The Understanding of Revelation in 'Dei Verbum' and the Response of Faith." *Homiletic and Pastoral Review*, June 11, 2014, 1–10. http://www.hprweb.com/2014/06/the-understanding-of-revelation-in-dei-verbum-and-the-response-of-faith/.

Bibliography

Greinacher, Norbert, and Virgilio Elizondo, eds. *The Transmission of Christian Faith to the Next Generation*. Edinburgh: T. & T. Clark, 1984.

Groome, Thomas H. *Sharing Faith: A Comprehensive Approach to Religious Education and Pastoral Ministry: The Way of Shared Praxis*. Eugene, OR: Wipf & Stock, 1998.

Gutiérrez, Gustavo. "Option for the Poor." In *An Eerdmans Reader in Contemporary Political Theology*, edited by William T. Cavanaugh et al., 174–93. Grand Rapids: Eerdmans, 2012.

———. *A Theology of Liberation: History, Politics, and Salvation*. 15th anniversary ed. Maryknoll: Orbis, 1988.

———. *We Drink from Our Own Wells*. Maryknoll: Orbis, 1988.

Hess, Ellen. H. "Contributions from New Forms of Consecrated Life for Initial Formation of Young Religious as Developed in the Verbum Dei Missionary Fraternity." STL thesis, Jesuit School of Theology at Berkeley, 2004.

Isasi-Díaz, Ada María. *La Lucha Continues: Mujerista Theology*. Maryknoll: Orbis, 2004.

Jaspers, Karl. "Communication: The Loving Struggle." In *Karl Jaspers: Basic Philosophical Writings*, edited by Edith Ehrlich et al., 73–79. Athens: Ohio University Press, 1986.

John Paul II. *Redemptoris Missio*. Encyclical on the Permanent Validity on the Church's Missionary Mandate, December 7, 1990. http://w2.vatican.va/content/john-paul-ii/en/encyclicals/documents/hf_jp-ii_enc_07121990_redemptoris-missio.html.

Kollman, Paul V. *The Evangelization of Slaves and Catholic Origins in Eastern Africa*. Maryknoll: Orbis, 2005.

Lankshear, Colin, and Peter McLaren, eds. *The Politics of Liberation: Paths from Freire*. New York: Routledge, 1994.

Lawlor, Antoine. "Ever Ancient, Ever New: The Art and Practice of *Lectio Divina*." United States Conference of Catholic Bishops. September 20, 2009. http://www.usccb.org/beliefs-and-teachings/how-we-teach/catechesis/catechetical-sunday/word-of-god/upload/lectio-divina.pdf.

Lenchak, Timothy. "The Function of the Bible in the Roman Catholic Mission." In *Scripture, Community, and Mission: Essays in Honor of D. Preman Niles*, edited by Philip L. Wickeri, 3–13. Hong Kong: Christian Conference of Asia, 2002.

Leonardo, Zeus. "Reality on Trial: Notes on Ideology, Education, and Utopia." *Policy Futures in Education* 1 (2003) 504–25.

Loomba, Ania. *Colonialism/Postcolonialism: The New Critical Idiom*. 3rd ed. New York: Routledge, 2005.

Louf, André. *In the School of Contemplation*. Collegeville: Liturgical, 2015.

Lukás, Georg. "Class Consciousness." In *Ideology*, edited by Terry Eagleton, 31–49. London: Routledge, 2013.

Luzbetak, Louis J. *The Church and Cultures: New Perspectives in Missiological Anthropology*. Maryknoll: Orbis, 1988.

Martin Rubio, Angel David. "La Persecucion Religiosa de 1936–1939: Estado de la Cuestion y Propuestas Historiograficas." *Hispania Sacra* 49 (1997) 43–71.

Masson, Joseph. "Legacy of Pierre Charles, SJ." *Occasional Bulletin of Missionary Research* 2 (1978) 118–20.

Mayo, Peter. *Gramsci, Freire and Adult Education: Possibilities for Transformative Action*. New York: Zed, 1999.

McAfee Brown, Robert. *Spirituality and Liberation: Overcoming the Great Fallacy*. Philadelphia: Westminster, 2001.

Bibliography

McLaren, Peter. *Life in Schools: An Introduction to Critical Pedagogy in the Foundations of Education.* 5th ed. Boston: Allyn and Bacon, 2007.

Merton, Thomas. *Contemplation in a World of Action.* Notre Dame: University of Notre Dame Press, 1998.

Morrow, Raymond Allen, and Carlos Alberto Torres. *Reading Freire and Habermas: Critical Pedagogy and Transformative Social Change.* New York: Teachers College Press, 2002.

Mounier, Emmanuel. *Personalism.* Notre Dame: University of Notre Dame Press, 1989.

Müller, Karl. "The Legacy of Joseph Schmidlin." *International Bulletin of Missionary Research* 4 (1980) 109–13.

Müller, Karl, et al., eds. *Dictionary of Mission: Theology, History, Perspectives.* Eugene, OR: Pickwick, 2006.

O'Brien, David J., and Thomas A. Shannon. *Catholic Social Thought: The Documentary Heritage.* Maryknoll: Orbis, 1992.

Paul VI. *Evangelii Nuntiandi.* Apostolic Exhortation on Evangelization in the Modern World, December 8, 1965. http://w2.vatican.va/content/paul-vi/en/apost_exhortations/documents/hf_p-vi_exh_19751208_evangelii-nuntiandi.html.

Pellegrino, Mary. "The Future Enters Us Long Before It Happens: Opening Space for an Emerging Narrative of Communion." Presidential address at the 2017 annual assembly of the Leadership Conference of Women's Religious, Orlando, FL, August 10, 2017.

Phan, Peter C. "The World Missionary Conference, Edinburgh 1910: Challenges for Church and Theology in the Twenty-First Century." *International Bulletin of Missionary Research* 34 (2010) 105–8.

Pontifical Council for Inter-Religious Dialogue. "Dialogue and Proclamation." Reflection and Orientations on Interreligious Dialogue and the Proclamation of the Gospel of Jesus Christ, May 19, 1991. http://www.vatican.va/roman_curia/pontifical_councils/interelg/documents/rc_pc_interelg_doc_19051991_dialogue-and-proclamatio_en.html.

Prinz, Julia D. E. *Endangering Hunger for God: Johann Baptist Metz and Dorothee Sölle at the Interface of Biblical Hermeneutic and Christian Spirituality.* Piscataway, NJ: LIT Verlag, 2007.

———. "Hermeneutics of Hunger: Part II; Dei Verbum #2, Ongoing Possibilities." Paper presented at the 77th international meeting at the Catholic Biblical Association, Providence College, RI, July 26–29, 2014.

Quitslund, Sonya A. "A Feminist Perspective on Kings and Kingdom." *Living Light* 19 (1982) 134–39.

Rahner, Karl. *The Trinity.* New York: Crossroad, 1997.

Ratzinger, Joseph. *Milestones: Memoirs 1927–1977.* Translated by Erasmo Leiva-Merikakis. San Francisco: Ignatius, 1998.

Rogoff, Barbara. *Apprenticeship in Thinking: Cognitive Development in Social Context.* New York: Oxford, 1990.

Rosales, Gaudencio, and C. G. Arevalo, eds. *FABC Documents from 1970–1991.* Vol. 1 of *For All the Peoples of Asia.* Manila: Claretian, 1997.

Rowland, Christopher, ed. *The Cambridge Companion to Liberation Theology.* Cambridge: Cambridge University Press, 1999.

Bibliography

Sartre, Jean-Paul. "Man Makes Himself." In *Reading for Philosophical Inquiry: A Brief Introduction to Philosophical Thinking ver. 0.21; An Open Source Reader*, edited by Lee Archie and John G. Archie, 278–302. Greenwood, SC: Lee Archie and John G. Archie, 2004. http://philosophy.lander.edu/intro/introbook.pdf.

Scherer, James A., and Stephen B. Bevans, eds. *Basic Statements 1974–1991*. Vol. 1 of *New Directions in Mission and Evangelization*. Maryknoll: Orbis, 1994.

———. *Theological Foundations*. Vol. 2 of *New Directions in Mission and Evangelization*. Maryknoll: Orbis, 1994.

Schipani, Daniel S. *Conscientization and Creativity: Paulo Freire and Christian Education*. Lanham, MD: University Press of America, 1984.

Schmitz, Josef, and Horzt Rzepkowski. "Missionary Methods." In Müller et al., *Dictionary of Mission*, 316–21.

Schreiter, Robert J. *Constructing Local Theologies*. Maryknoll: Orbis, 2002.

———. *The Ministry of Reconciliation: Spirituality and Strategies*. Maryknoll: Orbis, 1998.

———. *The New Catholicity: Theology between the Global and the Local*. Maryknoll: Orbis, 1997.

Scocuglia, Afonso Celso. *A História das Ideias de Paulo Freire e a Atual Crise de Paradigmas*. João Pessoa, Brazil: Editora Universitária, 1997.

Second Vatican Council. *Ad Gentes*. Decree on the Mission Activity of the Church, December 7, 1965. http://www.vatican.va/archive/hist_councils/ii_vatican_council/documents/vat-ii_decree_19651207_ad-gentes_en.html.

———. *Dei Verbum*. Dogmatic Constitution on Divine Revelation, November 18, 1965. http://www.vatican.va/archive/hist_councils/ii_vatican_council/documents/vat-ii_const_19651118_dei-verbum_en.html.

———. *Gaudium et Spes*. Pastoral Constitution on the Church in the Modern World, December 7, 1965. http://www.vatican.va/archive/hist_councils/ii_vatican_council/documents/vat-ii_const_19651207_gaudium-et-spes_en.html.

———. *Lumen Gentium*. Dogmatic Constitution on the Church, November 18, 1965. http://www.vatican.va/archive/hist_councils/ii_vatican_council/documents/vat-ii_const_19641121_lumen-gentium_en.html.

———. *Nostra Aetate*. Declaration on the Relation of the Church to Non-Christian Religions, October 28, 1965. http://www.vatican.va/archive/hist_councils/ii_vatican_council/documents/vat-ii_decl_19651028_nostra-aetate_en.html.

———. *Sacrosanctum Concilium*. Constitution on the Sacred Liturgy, December 4, 1965. http://www.vatican.va/archive/hist_councils/ii_vatican_council/documents/vat-ii_const_19631204_sacrosanctum-concilium_en.html.

Serpa, María de Lourdes B., and Caetano Serpa. Review of *Pedagogia da Autonomia: Saberes Necessários à Prática Educative*, by Paulo Freire. *Journal of Pedagogy, Pluralism, and Practice* 1 (1997) 16–19. http://www.lesley.edu/journal-pedagogy-pluralism-practice/maria-serpa-caetano-serpa/pedagogia-da-autonomia/?terms=%22Maria%20de%20Lourdes%20B.%20Serpa%22.

Shorter, Aylward. *Toward a Theology of Inculturation*. Eugene, OR: Wipf & Stock, 1999.

Sínodo de los Obispos. "La Nueva Evangelización para la Transmisión de la Fe Cristiana." Lineamenta de la XIII Asamblea General Ordinaria, February 2, 2011. http://www.vatican.va/roman_curia/synod/documents/rc_synod_doc_20110202_lineamenta-xiii-assembly_sp.html.

Bibliography

Skreslet, Stanley H. *Comprehending Mission: The Questions, Methods, Themes, Problems, and Prospects of Missiology.* American Society Mission Series 49. Maryknoll: Orbis, 2012.

Souza, Ana Inês. *Paulo Freire: Vida e Obra.* São Paulo: Editora Expressão Popular, 2001.

Spivak, Gayatri C. "Can the Subaltern Speak?" In *Can the Subaltern Speak? Reflections on the History of an Idea,* edited by Rosalind Morris, 21–80. New York: Colombia University, 2010.

Stanley, Brian. "The World Missionary Conference, Edinburgh 1910: Sifting History from Myth." *Touchstone* 28 (2010) 7–18.

———. *The World Missionary Conference, Edinburgh 1910: Studies in the History of Christian Missions.* Grand Rapids: Eerdmans, 2009.

Sundermeier, Theo. "Theology of Mission." In Müller et al., *Dictionary of Mission,* 429–51.

Synod of Bishops. "The New Evangelization for the Transmission of the Christian Faith." Lineamenta of the 13th Ordinary General Assembly of the Synod of Bishops, February 2, 2011. http://www.vatican.va/roman_curia/synod/documents/rc_synod_doc_20110202_lineamenta-xiii-assembly_en.html.

Vygotsky, Lev S. *Mind in Society: The Development of Higher Psychological Processes.* Cambridge: Harvard University Press.

Waaijman, Kees. *Spirituality: Forms, Foundations, Methods.* Dudley, MA: Peeters, 2002.

Walls, Andrew. "Christian Mission in a Five-Hundred-Year Context." Afterword to *Mission in the 21st Century: Exploring the Five Marks of Global Mission,* edited by Andrew Walls and Cathy Ross, 193–204. New York: Orbis, 2008.

Weiler, Kathleen. "The Myths of Paulo Freire." *Educational Theory* 46 (1996) 353–71.

Whiteman, Darrell. "Contextualization: The Theory, the Gap, the Challenge." *International Bulletin of Mission Research* 21 (1997) 2–7.

Williams, Thomas D., and Jan Olof Bengtsson. "Personalism." In *Stanford Encyclopedia of Philosophy,* edited by Edward N. Zalta. Last modified December 2, 2013. https://plato.stanford.edu/archives/sum2016/entries/personalism/.

Wojtyła, Karol. *Sources of Renewal: Study on the Implementation of the Second Vatican Council.* Translated by P. S. Falla. London: Collins, 1981.

Worrall, Simon. "Yes, Animals Think and Feel. Here's How We Know." *National Geographic,* July 15, 2015. https://news.nationalgeographic.com/2015/07/150714-animal-dog-thinking-feelings-brain-science/.

Zago, Marcello. "The New Millennium and the Emerging Religious Encounters." *Missiology: An International Review* 28 (2000) 5–18.

Index

accommodation, missionary, 66–67, 66n28
action, need for, 48, 50, 50n87
activism, 47
Ad Gentes (Decree on the Church's Missionary Activity), 4, 7, 119
agenda, for twenty-first century, 22–23
Allen, Roland, 61–62, 98
Amalados, Michael, 8
Amoris Laetitia (Frances, Pope, apostolic exhortation), 22
Anderson, Rufus, 61, 62
announcing, structures that will humanize, 51–52, 52n91
anthropological model, 16
anti-dialogue, 54–55
Arrupe, Pedro, 115n3
authentic dialogue, 50, 55, 57, 58
authoritarianism, 34

Balthasar, Hans Urs von, 3n6
banking education concept, 64n19
Barrett, David B., 21n77
believing, 72
Bernanos, Georges, 34
Bevans, Stephen B.
    background, 6–7
    common aspects with Freire's thought, 77–81
    contextual theology, 15–19, 25–26
    contribution to Verbum Dei's mission, 105–8
    on doing mission, 24–25, 112–13
    mission as dialogue, 10–12
    mission as prophecy, 12–15
    "Missionary Ecclesiology," 119
    Models of Contextual Theology, 6, 16
    prophetic dialogue (*See* prophetic dialogue)
    Prophetic Dialogue, 25
Bible
    dynamism of, 90–94
    use of, 86, 86n7, 89
Boff, Leonardo, 14
Bonet Bonet, Jaime
    on Apostle Paul's missionary life, 97–98
    author's personal experience with, 94n28
    background, 84–86, 95n30
    death of, 94n28
    dialogue with God, 94–96
    formulation of *Dei Verbum*, 85–89, 100
    "The Herald of the Evangelizer," 108–10, 108n52
    living the Gospel, 90, 90n20
    on love, 83, 83n1
    mission in weakness, 100
    missionary zeal, 97n34

Index

Bonet Bonet, Jaime *(continued)*
   power of love, 83
   on unity of body of Christ, 98–99n38
Bosch, David, 1, 5n16, 21–22, 22n79, 98
Bouyer, Louis, 3n6
Brazil, conditions in, 29–30, 29n7
Brown, Robert McAfee, 103–4n43

California's Latino immigrant population
   background, 101–2
   Good Friday service (St. Anthony's church), 19–20, 74–76
   VDME applied to, 103–5
Cámara, Helder, Dom, 35, 35n33
capitalism, 34
Charles, Pierre, 62–63
Chenu, Marie-Dominique, 3n6
Christianity, 33–34, 118
church
   as multi-centric, 118
   as a new community, 98
   relationship with the world, 99
   in twenty-first-century, 21–24, 112
   understanding of, 111–12
cognitive development, 49n83
Collins, Denis, 41, 43
colonialization, consequences of, 116, 116–17n4
communication function, 17–18
conation, term usage, 72
Congar, Yves, 2–3n6
conscientização
   description, 34–36
   dialogue and, 54–57
   Freire's aims of, 49–54, 58
   Freire's conception of, 27
   investigation, 41–42
   mutual learning process and, 75
   phases of, 41–44
   problematization, 43–44
   as a process, 57–58, 57n108, 76–77
   prophetic dialogue, common elements chart, 78
   prophetic dialogue, common elements diagram, 80
   prophetic dialogue, common elements with, 73–77

   prophetic dialogue, enhancement of, 60–61, 76
   reality, perception of, 44–49
   thermatization, 42–43
   Third World situation, 58
   utopia and, 52–53, 52–53n94
   why and how of, 36–44
consecrated life, new understanding of, 86–87, 86n7
contemplative life, 93–94n25
contextual theology, 15–19, 25–26
Contextual Theology Conference (2009), 22
contextualization, 66
corporal punishment, 37, 37n42
countercultural model, 16
critical pedagogy, 71–72, 71n46, 117
critical thinking, 71n46
cultural action, for liberation, 50
culture of dependence, 30

dechristianization, 21, 21n77
deep listening process, 74–75
Dei Verbum (Dogmatic Constitution on Divine Revelation), 85n5, 118
democracy, 55, 55n101
denouncing, dehumanizing structures, 51–52, 52n91
dependence, culture of, 30
develop function, 18
dialogue
   authentic, 50, 55, 57, 58
   Bevans on, 10–12
   conscientização and, 54–57
   dimensions, 55
   as foundation of mission, 9
   importance of, 75–76, 107
   prophetic (*See* prophetic dialogue)
   as spirituality, 10–11, 25
   for twenty-first century, 23–24
Dialogue and Proclamation (Pontifical Council document), 9, 10–11
"dialogue method," 13, 13n50
discipleship, spirituality and, 103–4n43
Donovan, Vincent, 61
dreams, 52–53, 52–53n94
Duff, Alexander, 61, 62

Index

Dynamism of the Word, 90–94, 91n22, 103–5, 106

economic Trinity, 12n43
ecumenical dialogue, 9–10
education
    for freedom, 49–50
    as an ontological vocation, 38
    poverty and, 28
Education as the Practice of Freedom (Freire), 29
empowerment, 87
enculturation, 65
environmental concerns, 22
eschatological convictions, of Apostle Paul, 99
Esquedra Bifet, Juan, 5n16
ethnocentrism, 65–66
Evangelii Gaudium (Francis, Pope apostolic exhortation), 9–10
Evangelii Nuntiandi (Paul VI's apostolic exhortation), 7, 96n31
"exist" vs. "live," 46, 46n70, 46n71, 48
existential necessity, dialogue as, 55–56
exploitation, 21

faith, transmission of, 67–73
family dynamics, 37–38, 37n42
Fanon, Frantz, 30
Faundez, Antonio, 57n106
Federation of Asian Bishops' Conferences (FABC), 12, 12n45
fellowship, 90
Francis, Pope, 9–10, 22, 69, 70, 106
Freire, Paulo
    arrest and exile of, 39–40, 39n48
    background, 28–29
    banking education concept, 64n19
    Christianity, 33–34
    common aspects with Bevans's thought, 77–81
    conscientização (See *conscientização*)
    contribution to Verbum Dei's mission, 105–8
    criticisms of, 117–18, 117–18n5
    death of, 59n110
    depression, suffering from, 38–39, 39n46
    existentialism, 31–32
    Marxism, 33
    personalism, 30–31
    phenomenology, 32
    philosophical influence, 29–34
    reality, understanding of, 44–49
    "spoken" books, 57n106
Freire, Paulo, publications
    Education as the Practice of Freedom, 29
    Pedagogy of Freedom, 58, 59n110, 60, 119–120
    Pedagogy of Hope, 36
    Pedagogy of Indignation, 111
    Pedagogy of the Oppressed, 29, 36, 40, 56n103
Fromm, Erich Seligmann, 30
functions of contextualization, 17–18

Geisel, Ernesto, 29n7
"generative words," 41
ghost, as missionary image, 65
global context, 24
"Global South," 16n62
God's imminent triumph, mission in context of, 99
God's will, doing, 72
Good Friday service (St. Anthony's church), 19–20, 74–76
Goulart, Joao, 30
Gramsci, Antonio, 30
Groome, Thomas H., 68, 68n34, 70–73, 81
guest, as missionary image, 64
Gutiérrez, Gustavo, 14, 103n143

Harvard Graduate School of Education (HGSE), 59n110
healing process, 74–75
Heidegger, Martin, 31, 47n76, 71n44
Heller, Agnes, 30
"The Herald of the Evangelizer" (Bonet Bonet), 108–9, 108n52
Hindu-Christian approaches to theology, 4

Index

historical awareness of mission methods, 61–67
historical commitment, 53–54
History and Class Consciousness (Lukács), 33
hominization, political action for, 48
human beings
    existence as a task of praxis, 47
    ontological vocation, 38, 47–48n76
    relationships with the world, 45–46
    as unfinished beings, 47, 58–59
    vocation, to become a subject, 47–48
human dignity, 31
humanism, 30

immanent Trinity, 12n43
immigrant populations
    background, 101–2
    census data, 102n42
    Good Friday service (St. Anthony's church), 19–20, 74–76
    VDME applied to, 103–5
incarnation, 66–67
inculturation, 66, 69n39
interreligious dialogue, 9–11
investigation phase, 41–42

Jaspers, Karl, 56
John Paul II, Pope, 7, 84n2
Johnson, Todd M., 21n77

kingdom of God, 67n31
Kosik, Karel, 30
Kurian, George T., 21n77

Lara, Alvares, 84n2
Latin American Episcopal Conference (1968), 4
lectio divina, 90–91, 90–91n21
liberation
    cultural action for, 50
    of educating processes, 49n82
    role in missionary strategy, 63
liberation pedagogy, 59n110
liberation spirituality, 103–4n43
liberation theology, 4, 14, 34
Lima, Alceu Amoroso, 33

"limit-situations," 36, 36n39, 43, 48n80
listening
    deep listening process, 74–75
    prophecy and, 13
    Word of God, 106
literacy, acquiring, 50
literacy program phases, 41–44
"live" vs. "exist," 46, 46n70, 46n71, 48
local churches, selfhood of, 98
local cultural identities, 21
locus theologicus, 17
Loomba, Ania, 116–17n4
Louvain school of thought, 62–63
Lukács, György, 30, 33
Lumen Fidei (Francis, Pope, encyclical), 69, 106
Lumen Gentium (Dogmatic Constitution on the Church), 3–4, 85n5
Luzbetak, Louis J., 5n16, 65–66, 65n22, 81

Macedo, Donaldo, 59n110
magic consciousness, 41–42
Maritain, Jacques, 34
marriage and family, 22–23
Marx, Karl, 30
Marxism, 33
McConnell, Doug, 11
Memmi, Albert, 30
Merton, Thomas, 93n25
method of dialogue, twenty-first century, 23
migrant worker, as missionary image, 65
mission
    Apostle Paul's missionary paradigm of, 98–99
    concept of, 112
    as dialogue, 10–12
    general understanding of, 4–5
    historical awareness of methods, 61–67
    images of methods, 64–65
    as multi-centric, 118
    Paul VI, Pope, 2, 2n4
    as prophecy, 12–15
    as prophetic dialogue, 7–10
    in weakness, 99–100

Index

missional ecclesiology, 119, 119n8
missionary accommodation, 66–67, 66n28
"Missionary Ecclesiology" (Bevans and Schroeder), 119
Missionary Methods (Allen), 98
Models of Contextual Theology (Bevans), 6, 16
Mounier, Emmanuel, 31, 34
Münster school of thought, 63
mutual learning process, 75

neoliberalism, 34
The New Evangelization for the Transmission of the Christian Faith (Synod of Bishops document), 69–70, 96
Nostra Aetate (Declaration on the Relation of the Church to Non-Christian Religions), 2n4, 4

offend function, 18
Oman, John Wood, 6
ontological enterprise, faith as, 72–73
ontological vocation, 38, 47–48n76
ontology, in a Heideggerian sense of "being," 71n44
oppression
  denouncing and announcing, 51–52, 52n91
  Freire's exile, 39–40
  liberation spirituality, 103–4n43
  living and existing, 46
  mission and, 116
  political power and, 49–50
  poverty and, 36, 36n38
  structures of, 21

Panikkar, Raimon, 4
partner, as missionary image, 65
paternalism, 66n25
Paul, Apostle, 97–100
Paul VI, Pope, 2, 2n4, 7, 12n45, 14, 96n31
Pedagogy of Freedom (Freire), 58, 59n110, 60, 119–120
Pedagogy of Hope (Freire), 36
Pedagogy of Indignation (Freire), 111

Pedagogy of the Oppressed (Freire), 29, 36, 40, 56n103
Pernia, Antonio, 6n21
personalism, 30–31
Phan, Peter C., 2
phenomenology, 32
Piaget, Jean, 37
Pius XII, Pope, 84
pluralistic religious world, 21
political action for hominization, 48
Pontifical Council for Interreligious Dialogue, 10–11
Populorum Progressio (Paul VI encyclical), 14
poverty
  education and, 28
  family dynamics and, 37–38
  liberation theology and, 14, 63
praxis model, 16, 47
Prinz, Julia, 89, 91
problematization phase, 43, 43–44n58
prophecy
  denouncing and announcing, 51–52, 52n91
  mission as, 12–15
prophet as missionary image, 64
prophetic dialogue
  concept of, 7–10, 112
  conscientização, common elements chart, 78
  conscientização, common elements diagram, 80
  conscientização, common elements with, 73–77
  conscientização, enhancement of, 60–61, 76
  contextual theology and, 15–19, 25–26
  exercising, 19–21
  mission as, 7–10
  mutual learning process and, 75
  as a process, 76–77
  twenty-first-century church and, 21–24
  voices and, 23
Prophetic Dialogue (Bevans & Schroeder), 25

133

Index

Protestant missiologists, 61–62, 119n8

racism, 66n25
Rahner, Karl, 12n43, 89
reality, Freire's understanding, 44–49
Redemptoris Missio (John Paul II's encyclical), 7
reign of God, 67n31
ressourcement movement, 2–3n6
revelation, concept of, 105–6, 114
Roman Catholic Church
    catholicity of, 3, 3n8
    dialogue as foundation of mission, 9
    mission theology, 112
    missionary strategy, 62–63
    salvation outside of the church, 2n4
    Spanish government and, 95n30
    . *See also* Vatican Council II
Rzepkowski, Horzt, 62

Sacrosanctum Concilium (Constitution on the Sacred Liturgy), 4
Sartre, Jean-Paul, 30, 32, 47–48n76
Schmidlin, Joseph, 63n13
Schmitz, Josef, 62
Schreiter, Robert J., 3n8, 15–16
Scripture. *See* Bible, use of
Second Vatican Council. *See* Vatican Council II
sectarianism, 36
secularization, 21
"Seeing Mission through Images" (Bevans), 63
Serviço Social da Indústria (SESI), 37–39
Shared Christian praxis, 70–71, 70n43
Shor, Ira, 57n106
Shorter, Aylward, 69n39
slavery, 61
snowball system, 98–99n38
Sobrino, Jon, 14
social learning, 49n83
society, mission and transformation of, 99
Society of the Divine Word (SVD), 6
solipsism, 45
Spanish government, Catholic Church and, 95n30

spirituality, liberation, 103–4n43
spirituality dimension in dialogue, 10–11, 25
Spivak, Gayatri Chakravorty, 116–17n4
"spoken" books, 57n106
stranger, as missionary image, 64
suffering, 38–39, 76
Suquia, Angel, 84n2
synthetic model, 16

teachers and teaching
    as missionary image, 64
    mutual learning process, 75
    as an ontological vocation, 38
thematic investigation phase, 42–43
"thematic universe," 42
theology, mission and, 25–26
theory, 71n46
Third World
    churches, 15–16
    political and economic situation, 58
    theologies, 21
thought-language, 45, 49
time, commitment in, 53–54
totalitarian ideologies, 31
transcendental model, 16
transformation, personal and social, 80
Transforming Mission (Bosch), 21
translational model, 16
treasure hunter, as missionary image, 64
Trinity, 12n43
Tristão de Ataíde, 33
triumphalism, 66n25
trusting, 72
"truth encounter," 11

understanding, process of, 75
utopia, *conscientização* and, 52–53, 52–53n94

Vatican Council II
    church, understanding of, 111–12
    consecration, new understanding of, 86n7
    mission, understanding of, 2–5, 63
    role of women, 87n10
    salvation outside of the church, 2n4

Index

Vatican Council II documents
    Ad Gentes, 4, 7, 119
    Dei Verbum, 3–4, 118
    Lumen Gentium, 3–4, 85n5
    Nostra Aetate, 2n4, 4
    Sacrosanctum Concilium, 4
verbalism, 47
Verbum Dei Missionary Fraternity (VDMF)
    Bevans's contributions, 105–8
    California's Latino immigrant population and, 19–20, 74–76, 101–5
    central element in, 90–96
    charism and mission of, 83–90, 84n2, 84n5, 115–16
    Constitution, 84–85n3, 86n7, 88n12, 89, 93n24
    Dynamism of the Word, 90–94, 91n22, 103–5, 106
    Freire's contributions, 105–8
    global reach of, 97–98n34
    growing area in, 86n7
    multicultural activities, 105n47

    three branches, 86
Viana, Enciso, 84n2
"vocabulary universe," 41
voices, prophetic dialogue and, 23
Vygotsky, Lev, 49n83

Walls, Andrew, 118
Weil, Simone, 30
Wheel of Metanoia, 91–94
Whiteman, Darrell, 17–18
wisdom, conation and, 72
women
    experience of subaltern women, 116–17n4
    role of, 86–87, 87n9, 87n10
    in VDMF, 87n9
Word of God
    listening and, 106
    prayer and, 90–94, 91n22
    relationship with, 94–96
World Missionary Conference (1910), 62

Zago, Marcello, 13n50

www.ingramcontent.com/pod-product-compliance
Lightning Source LLC
Chambersburg PA
CBHW051942160426
43198CB00013B/2266